AIR FRYER
COOKBOOK *for Beginners*

1700 Days of Crispy, Flavorful, and Simple Recipes to Transform Your Everyday Meals | Fry, Bake, Grill & Roast

John Thomas

All Rights Reserved.

The contents of this book may not be reproduced, copied or transmitted without the direct written permission of the author or publisher. Under no circumstances will the publisher or the author be held responsible or liable for any damage, compensation or pecuniary loss arising directly or indirectly from the information contained in this book.

Legal notice. This book is protected by copyright. It is intended for personal use only. You may not modify, distribute, sell, use, quote or paraphrase any part or content of this book without the consent of the author or publisher.

Notice Of Disclaimer.

Please note that the information in this document is intended for educational and entertainment purposes only. Every effort has been made to provide accurate, up-to-date, reliable and complete information. No warranty of any kind is declared or implied. The reader acknowledges that the author does not engage in the provision of legal, financial, medical or professional advice. The content in this book has been obtained from a variety of sources. Please consult a licensed professional before attempting any of the techniques described in this book. By reading this document, the reader agrees that in no event shall the author be liable for any direct or indirect damages, including but not limited to errors, omissions or inaccuracies, resulting from the use of the information in this document.

CONTENTS

INTRODUCTION 1

Bread And Breakfast 2

Blueberry Pannenkoek (dutch Pancake) 2
Hole In One 2
Pesto Egg & Ham Sandwiches 2
French Toast And Turkey Sausage Roll-ups 3
Sweet Potato-cinnamon Toast 3
Scotch Eggs 3
Spring Vegetable Omelet 4
Western Frittata 4
Flank Steak With Caramelized Onions 4
Classic Cinnamon Rolls 5
Blueberry Muffins 5
Scones 5
Smooth Walnut-banana Loaf 6
Pigs In A Blanket 6
Broccoli Cornbread 6
Breakfast Pot Pies 7
Ham & Cheese Sandwiches 7
Sugar-dusted Beignets 7
Crispy Chicken Cakes 8
Baked Eggs With Bacon-tomato Sauce 8

Sandwiches And Burgers Recipes 8

Philly Cheesesteak Sandwiches 8
Sausage And Pepper Heros 9
Chili Cheese Dogs 9
Chicken Club Sandwiches 10
Dijon Thyme Burgers 10
Lamb Burgers 11
Thanksgiving Turkey Sandwiches 11
Chicken Apple Brie Melt 12
Mexican Cheeseburgers 12
Asian Glazed Meatballs 12
Perfect Burgers 13
Inside-out Cheeseburgers 13
Eggplant Parmesan Subs 14
Salmon Burgers 14

Thai-style Pork Sliders 15
Best-ever Roast Beef Sandwiches 15
Black Bean Veggie Burgers 16
Inside Out Cheeseburgers 16
Crunchy Falafel Balls 16
Reuben Sandwiches 17

Appetizers And Snacks 17

Crispy Ravioli Bites 17
Crab Rangoon 18
Crabby Fries 18
Savory Sausage Balls 19
Tomato & Basil Bruschetta 19
Bacon & Blue Cheese Tartlets 19
Nicoise Deviled Eggs 20
Chili Black Bean Empanadas 20
Turkey Spring Rolls 20
Cocktail Beef Bites 21
Rosemary Garlic Goat Cheese 21
Fried Brie With Cherry Tomatoes 21
Individual Pizzas 22
Thai-style Crab Wontons 22
Cholula Avocado Fries 22
Cheese Straws 23
Mozzarella Sticks 23
Kale Chips 23
Poppy Seed Mini Hot Dog Rolls 24
Crispy Tofu Bites 24

Poultry Recipes 24

Japanese-style Turkey Meatballs 24
Crispy Cordon Bleu 25
Indian Chicken Tandoori 25
Gruyère Asparagus & Chicken Quiche 25
Asian Meatball Tacos 26
Mexican-inspired Chicken Breasts 26
Fiesta Chicken Plate 27
Kale & Rice Chicken Rolls 27
Chicken Meatballs With A Surprise 27
Cajun Fried Chicken 28

Recipe	Page
Creole Chicken Drumettes	28
Buffalo Egg Rolls	28
Teriyaki Chicken Legs	29
Curried Chicken Legs	29
Chicken Schnitzel Dogs	29
Chicken Breast Burgers	30
Crispy Chicken Parmesan	30
Bacon & Chicken Flatbread	31
Sweet Nutty Chicken Breasts	31
Chicken Rochambeau	31
Basic Chicken Breasts	32
Maewoon Chicken Legs	32
Jerk Turkey Meatballs	32
Parmesan Chicken Fingers	33
Italian Roasted Chicken Thighs	33
Sunday Chicken Skewers	34
Chicken & Rice Sautée	34
Cornish Hens With Honey-lime Glaze	34
Family Chicken Fingers	35
Cajun Chicken Livers	35

Fish And Seafood Recipes 35

Recipe	Page
Shrimp	35
Salty German-style Shrimp Pancakes	36
Buttered Swordfish Steaks	36
Crab Stuffed Salmon Roast	36
Breaded Parmesan Perch	37
Fish Nuggets With Broccoli Dip	37
Mediterranean Salmon Cakes	37
Fish Tortillas With Coleslaw	38
Sea Bass With Fruit Salsa	38
Hot Calamari Rings	38
Caribbean Jerk Cod Fillets	39
Stuffed Shrimp	39
Halibut With Coleslaw	39
Restaurant-style Breaded Shrimp	40
Five Spice Red Snapper With Green Onions And Orange Salsa	40
Honey Pecan Shrimp	40
Aromatic Ahi Tuna Steaks	41
Lobster Tails With Lemon Garlic Butter	41
Sea Bass With Potato Scales And Caper Aïoli	42
Mediterranean Cod Croquettes	42
Horseradish Crusted Salmon	42
Maple-crusted Salmon	43
Mojito Fish Tacos	43
Tex-mex Fish Tacos	43
Horseradish Tuna Croquettes	44
Firecracker Popcorn Shrimp	44
Garlic-lemon Steamer Clams	44
Peanut-crusted Salmon	45
Crispy Sweet-and-sour Cod Fillets	45
Creole Tilapia With Garlic Mayo	45

Beef, Pork & Lamb Recipes 46

Recipe	Page
Tandoori Lamb Samosas	46
T-bone Steak With Roasted Tomato, Corn And Asparagus Salsa	46
Sriracha Short Ribs	47
Tamari-seasoned Pork Strips	47
Seedy Rib Eye Steak Bites	47
Kawaii Pork Roast	47
Chorizo & Veggie Bake	48
Sirloin Steak Bites With Gravy	48
Honey Mustard Pork Roast	48
Crispy Lamb Shoulder Chops	49
Beef Brazilian Empanadas	49
Meat Loaves	49
Herby Lamb Chops	50
Tuscan Chimichangas	50
Balsamic Beef & Veggie Skewers	50
Cowboy Rib Eye Steak	51
Pepperoni Bagel Pizzas	51
Easy-peasy Beef Sliders	51
Kielbasa Chunks With Pineapple & Peppers	52
Crispy Pork Pork Escalopes	52
Creamy Horseradish Roast Beef	52
Barbecue Country-style Pork Ribs	53
Indonesian Pork Satay	53
Crispy Ham And Eggs	53
Pork Cutlets With Almond-lemon Crust	54
Crispy Pork Medallions With Radicchio And Endive Salad	54
Baby Back Ribs	55
Oktoberfest Bratwursts	55
Air-fried Roast Beef With Rosemary Roasted Potatoes	55
Effortless Beef & Rice	56

Vegetarian Recipes 56

Recipe	Page
Green Bean & Baby Potato Mix	56
Honey Pear Chips	57

- Stuffed Portobellos 57
- Caprese-style Sandwiches 57
- Veggie Burgers 58
- Meatless Kimchi Bowls 58
- Curried Potato, Cauliflower And Pea Turnovers 58
- Tandoori Paneer Naan Pizza 59
- Tomato & Squash Stuffed Mushrooms 59
- Thai Peanut Veggie Burgers 60
- Spicy Vegetable And Tofu Shake Fry 60
- Golden Fried Tofu 61
- Gorgeous Jalapeño Poppers 61
- Bengali Samosa With Mango Chutney 61
- Asparagus, Mushroom And Cheese Soufflés 62
- Vietnamese Gingered Tofu 62
- Powerful Jackfruit Fritters 63
- Spaghetti Squash And Kale Fritters With Pomodoro Sauce 63
- Basil Green Beans 63
- Sushi-style Deviled Eggs 64

Vegetable Side Dishes Recipes 64

- Mushrooms 64
- Fried Pearl Onions With Balsamic Vinegar And Basil 64
- Layered Mixed Vegetables 65
- Asparagus Wrapped In Pancetta 65
- Zucchini Boats With Ham And Cheese 65
- Patatas Bravas 66
- Onions 66
- Greek-inspired Ratatouille 66
- Sweet Potato Fries 67
- Almond Green Beans 67
- Lovely Mac'n'cheese 67

- Corn On The Cob 68
- Southern Okra Chips 68
- Blistered Green Beans 68
- Veggie Fritters 69
- Simple Peppered Carrot Chips 69
- Mediterranean Roasted Vegetables 69
- Cheesy Texas Toast 69
- Hawaiian Brown Rice 70
- Honey-mustard Asparagus Puffs 70

Desserts And Sweets 71

- Strawberry Donuts 71
- Carrot-oat Cake Muffins 71
- Almond-roasted Pears 71
- Bananas Foster Bread Pudding 72
- Cherry Cheesecake Rolls 72
- Chocolate Rum Brownies 72
- Tortilla Fried Pies 72
- Grilled Pineapple Dessert 73
- Healthy Chickpea Cookies 73
- Spiced Fruit Skewers 73
- Peanut Butter Cup Doughnut Holes 74
- Boston Cream Donut Holes 74
- Healthy Berry Crumble 75
- Coconut Rice Cake 75
- Lemon Pound Cake Bites 75
- Black And Blue Clafoutis 76
- Dark Chocolate Peanut Butter S'mores 76
- Apple & Blueberry Crumble 76
- Fast Brownies 77
- Banana Bread Cake 77

INDEX 78

INTRODUCTION

New to air frying? Don't worry! "Air Fryer Cookbook for Beginners" is here to guide you through 1700 days of crispy, flavorful, and simple recipes that will transform your everyday meals.

Why Choose Our Cookbook?

☑ Beginner-Friendly: Step-by-step instructions make air frying accessible to everyone, even if you've never used an air fryer before!

☑ Versatile Cooking Methods: Learn how to fry, bake, grill, and roast with your air fryer, expanding your culinary horizons.

☑ Time-Saving Wonder: Most recipes can be prepared in 30 minutes or less, perfect for busy lifestyles.

☑ Healthier Alternatives: Enjoy your favorite fried foods with up to 80% less fat, without compromising on taste or texture.

Inside, you'll find an incredible variety of recipes, including:

🥖 Bread And Breakfast

🥟 Appetizers And Snacks

🥗 Vegetable Side Dishes Recipes

🐟 Fish And Seafood Recipes

🥩 Beef, pork & Lamb Recipes

🍗 Poultry Recipes

🥬 Vegetarians Recipes

🍰 Desserts And Sweets

Unlock the power of your Air Fryer with this comprehensive collection of recipes.

Ready to start your air frying journey? Click "Add to Cart" now and transform your everyday meals into crispy, flavorful delights!

Bread And Breakfast

Blueberry Pannenkoek (dutch Pancake)

Servings: 4 | Prep Time: 5 Minutes | Cooking Time: 30 Minutes

Ingredients:

- 3 eggs, beaten
- ½ cup buckwheat flour
- ½ cup milk
- ½ tsp vanilla
- 1 ½ cups blueberries, crushed
- 2 tbsp powdered sugar

Directions:

1. Preheat air fryer to 165°C/330°F.
2. Mix together eggs, buckwheat flour, milk, and vanilla in a bowl.
3. Pour the batter into a greased baking pan and add it to the fryer.
4. Bake until the pancake is puffed and golden, 12-16 minutes.
5. Remove pan and flip pancake over onto a plate.
6. Top with crushed blueberries and powdered sugar. Serve.

Variations & Ingredients Tips:

- Use a cast iron or oven-safe skillet instead of a baking pan.
- Add lemon zest or cinnamon to the batter.
- Top with maple syrup or fruit compote.

Per Serving: Calories: 170; Total Fat: 3g; Saturated Fat: 1g; Cholesterol: 110mg; Sodium: 45mg; Total Carbs: 30g; Dietary Fiber: 3g; Total Sugars: 9g; Protein: 6g

Hole In One

Servings: 1 | Prep Time: 5 Minutes | Cooking Time: 7 Minutes

Ingredients:

- 1 slice bread
- 1 teaspoon soft butter
- 1 egg
- salt and pepper
- 1 tablespoon shredded Cheddar cheese
- 2 teaspoons diced ham

Directions:

1. Place a 15 x 15 cm baking dish inside air fryer basket and preheat fryer to 165°C/330°F.
2. Using a 6.4 cm-diameter biscuit cutter, cut a hole in center of bread slice.
3. Spread softened butter on both sides of bread.
4. Lay bread slice in baking dish and crack egg into the hole. Sprinkle egg with salt and pepper to taste.
5. Cook for 5 minutes.
6. Turn toast over and top it with shredded cheese and diced ham.
7. Cook for 2 more minutes or until yolk is done to your liking.

Variations & Ingredients Tips:

- Use bagels, English muffins or biscuits instead of bread.
- Add some sliced avocado, smoked salmon or sautéed spinach on top.
- Sprinkle with everything bagel seasoning or chopped chives for extra flavor.

Per Serving: Calories: 293; Total Fat: 18g; Saturated Fat: 8g; Cholesterol: 215mg; Sodium: 569mg; Total Carbs: 19g; Dietary Fiber: 1g; Total Sugars: 2g; Protein: 14g

Pesto Egg & Ham Sandwiches

Servings: 2 | Prep Time: 10 Minutes | Cooking Time: 20 Minutes

Ingredients:

- 4 sandwich bread slices
- 2 tbsp butter, melted
- 4 eggs, scrambled
- 4 deli ham slices
- 2 Colby cheese slices
- 4 tsp basil pesto sauce
- ¼ tsp red chili flakes
- ¼ avocado, sliced

Directions:

1. Preheat air fryer at 190°C/370°F.
2. Brush 2 pieces of bread with half of the butter and place them, butter side down, into the frying basket. Divide eggs, chili flakes, sliced avocado, ham, and cheese on each bread slice.
3. Spread pesto on the remaining bread slices and place them, pesto side-down, onto the sandwiches. Brush the remaining butter on the tops of the sandwiches and Bake for 6 minutes, flipping once. Serve immediately.

Variations & Ingredients Tips:

- Use different cheese like cheddar or Swiss.
- Add sliced tomatoes or sautéed mushrooms.
- Substitute pesto with sundried tomato spread or olive tapenade.

Per Serving: Calories: 599; Total Fat: 39g; Saturated Fat: 16g; Cholesterol: 436mg; Sodium: 1176mg; Total Carbohydrates: 32g; Dietary Fiber: 4g; Total Sugars: 3g; Protein: 29g

French Toast And Turkey Sausage Roll-ups

Servings: 3 | Prep Time: 10 Minutes | Cooking Time: 24 Minutes

Ingredients:

- 6 links turkey sausage
- 6 slices of white bread, crusts removed*
- 2 eggs
- 118 ml milk
- ½ teaspoon ground cinnamon
- ½ teaspoon vanilla extract
- 1 tablespoon butter, melted
- powdered sugar (optional)
- maple syrup

Directions:

1. Preheat the air fryer to 190°C/380°F and pour a little water into the bottom of the air fryer drawer. (This will help prevent the grease that drips into the bottom drawer from burning and smoking.)
2. Air-fry the sausage links at 190°C/380°F for 8 to 10 minutes, turning them a couple of times during the cooking process. (If you have pre-cooked sausage links, omit this step.)
3. Roll each sausage link in a piece of bread, pressing the finished seam tightly to seal shut.
4. Preheat the air fryer to 190°C/370°F.
5. Combine the eggs, milk, cinnamon, and vanilla in a shallow dish. Dip the sausage rolls in the egg mixture and let them soak in the egg for 30 seconds. Spray or brush the bottom of the air fryer basket with oil and transfer the sausage rolls to the basket, seam side down.
6. Air-fry the rolls at 190°C/370°F for 9 minutes. Brush melted butter over the bread, flip the rolls over and air-fry for an additional 5 minutes. Remove the French toast roll-ups from the basket and dust with powdered sugar, if using. Serve with maple syrup and enjoy.

Variations & Ingredients Tips:

- Use pork or veggie sausage instead of turkey for different flavors.
- Stuff the rolls with a slice of cheese before air frying for a gooey filling.
- Sprinkle with chopped nuts, coconut flakes or mini chocolate chips for extra texture.

Per Serving: Calories: 416; Total Fat: 24g; Saturated Fat: 8g; Cholesterol: 185mg; Sodium: 799mg; Total Carbs: 31g; Dietary Fiber: 1g; Total Sugars: 7g; Protein: 19g

Sweet Potato-cinnamon Toast

Servings: 6 | Prep Time: 5 Minutes | Cooking Time: 8 Minutes

Ingredients:

- 1 small sweet potato, cut into 1-cm slices
- Oil for misting
- Ground cinnamon

Directions:

1. Preheat air fryer to 200°C/390°F.
2. Spray sweet potato slices with oil on both sides.
3. Sprinkle both sides with cinnamon to taste.
4. Arrange slices in single layer in air fryer basket.
5. Cook 4 minutes, flip and cook 4 more minutes until barely fork tender.

Variations & Ingredients Tips:

- Use a mixture of cinnamon and brown sugar for coating.
- Drizzle with honey or maple syrup after cooking.
- Top with nut butter, chopped nuts or fresh fruit.

Per Serving: Calories: 28; Total Fat: 0g; Saturated Fat: 0g; Cholesterol: 0mg; Sodium: 13mg; Total Carbs: 6g; Dietary Fiber: 1g; Total Sugars: 2g; Protein: 0g

Scotch Eggs

Servings: 4 | Prep Time: 20 Minutes | Cooking Time: 25 Minutes

Ingredients:

- 2 tbsp flour, plus extra for coating
- 450g ground breakfast sausage
- 4 hardboiled eggs, peeled
- 1 raw egg
- 1 tbsp water
- Oil for misting or cooking spray
- Crumb Coating
- ¾ cup panko breadcrumbs
- ¾ cup flour

Directions:

1. Combine 2 tbsp flour with ground sausage and mix thoroughly.
2. Divide into 4 equal portions and mold each around a hard boiled egg to cover completely.
3. In a bowl, beat raw egg and water together.
4. Dip sausage-covered eggs in remaining flour, then egg mixture, then roll in crumb coating.
5. Cook at 180°C/360°F for 10 minutes. Spray eggs, turn, and spray other side.
6. Continue cooking for 15 more minutes or until sausage is well done.

Variations & Ingredients Tips:

- Use turkey or plant-based sausage for a lighter option.
- Add dried herbs or spices to the sausage for extra flavor.
- Serve with mustards, hot sauce or chutney for dipping.

Per Serving: Calories: 515; Total Fat: 33g; Saturated Fat: 11g; Cholesterol: 305mg; Sodium: 950mg; Total Carbs: 30g;

Dietary Fiber: 1g; Total Sugars: 2g; Protein: 24g

Spring Vegetable Omelet

Servings: 4 | Prep Time: 5 Minutes | Cooking Time: 20 Minutes

Ingredients:

- ¼ cup chopped broccoli, lightly steamed
- ½ cup grated cheddar cheese
- 6 eggs
- ¼ cup steamed kale
- 1 green onion, chopped
- Salt and pepper to taste

Directions:

1. Preheat air fryer to 180°C/360°F.
2. In a bowl, beat the eggs.
3. Stir in kale, broccoli, green onion, and cheddar cheese.
4. Transfer the mixture to a greased baking dish and bake in the air fryer for 15 minutes until golden and crisp.
5. Season to taste and serve immediately.

Variations & Ingredients Tips:

- Add diced ham, bacon or sausage for extra protein.
- Use different greens like spinach or arugula.
- Top with salsa, avocado or hot sauce.

Per Serving: Calories: 175; Total Fat: 11g; Saturated Fat: 4g; Cholesterol: 342mg; Sodium: 235mg; Total Carbs: 4g; Dietary Fiber: 1g; Total Sugars: 2g; Protein: 15g

Western Frittata

Servings: 1 | Prep Time: 10 Minutes | Cooking Time: 19 Minutes

Ingredients:

- ½ red or green bell pepper, cut into 1.3cm chunks
- 1 teaspoon olive oil
- 3 eggs, beaten
- ¼ cup grated Cheddar cheese
- ¼ cup diced cooked ham
- salt and freshly ground black pepper, to taste
- 1 teaspoon butter
- 1 teaspoon chopped fresh parsley

Directions:

1. Preheat the air fryer to 200°C/400°F.
2. Toss the peppers with the olive oil and air-fry for 6 minutes, shaking the basket once or twice during the cooking process to redistribute the ingredients.
3. While the vegetables are cooking, beat the eggs well in a bowl, stir in the Cheddar cheese and ham, and season with salt and freshly ground black pepper. Add the air-fried peppers to this bowl when they have finished cooking.
4. Place a 15cm or 18cm non-stick metal cake pan into the air fryer basket with the butter using an aluminum sling to lower the pan into the basket. (Fold a piece of aluminum foil into a strip about 5cm wide by 60cm long.)
5. Air-fry for 1 minute at 190°C/380°F to melt the butter. Remove the cake pan and rotate the pan to distribute the butter and grease the pan. Pour the egg mixture into the cake pan and return the pan to the air fryer, using the aluminum sling.
6. Air-fry at 190°C/380°F for 12 minutes, or until the frittata has puffed up and is lightly browned. Let the frittata sit in the air fryer for 5 minutes to cool to an edible temperature and set up. Remove the cake pan from the air fryer, sprinkle with parsley and serve immediately.

Variations & Ingredients Tips:

- Add sauteed mushrooms, spinach or other veggies to the egg mixture.
- Use feta or goat cheese instead of cheddar.
- Serve with salsa, avocado or hot sauce on top.

Per Serving: Calories: 435; Total Fat: 29g; Saturated Fat: 11g; Cholesterol: 535mg; Sodium: 865mg; Total Carbs: 7g; Dietary Fiber: 1g; Total Sugars: 3g; Protein: 33g

Flank Steak With Caramelized Onions

Servings: 2 | Prep Time: 10 Minutes | Cooking Time: 30 Minutes

Ingredients:

- 227 g flank steak, cubed
- 1 tablespoon mustard powder
- ½ teaspoon garlic powder
- 2 eggs
- 1 onion, sliced thinly
- Salt and pepper to taste

Directions:

1. Preheat air fryer to 180°C/360°F. Coat the flank steak cubes with mustard and garlic powders. Place them in the frying basket along with the onion and Bake for 3 minutes. Flip the steak over and gently stir the onions and cook for another 3 minutes. Push the steak and onions over to one side of the basket, creating space for heat-safe baking dish. Crack the eggs into a ceramic dish. Place the dish in the fryer. Cook for 15 minutes at 160°C/320°F until the egg white are set and the onion is caramelized. Season with salt and pepper. Serve warm.

Variations & Ingredients Tips:

- Use sirloin, ribeye or tenderloin instead of flank steak.
- Add some sliced bell peppers or mushrooms to the onions.
- Top with crumbled blue cheese or goat cheese for a creamy element.

Per Serving: Calories: 426; Total Fat: 25g; Saturated Fat: 9g; Cholesterol: 328mg; Sodium: 263mg; Total Carbs: 10g; Dietary Fiber: 1g; Total Sugars: 4g; Protein: 41g

Classic Cinnamon Rolls

Servings: 4 | Prep Time: 15 Minutes | Cooking Time: 6 Minutes

Ingredients:

- 1½ cups all-purpose flour
- 1 tablespoon granulated sugar
- 2 teaspoons baking powder
- ½ teaspoon salt
- 4 tablespoons butter, divided
- ½ cup buttermilk
- 2 tablespoons brown sugar
- 1 teaspoon cinnamon
- 1 cup powdered sugar
- 2 tablespoons milk

Directions:

1. Preheat the air fryer to 180°C/360°F.
2. In a large bowl, stir together the flour, sugar, baking powder, and salt. Cut in 3 tablespoons of the butter with a pastry blender or two knives until coarse crumbs remain. Stir in the buttermilk until a dough forms.
3. Place the dough onto a floured surface and roll out into a square shape about 1.25 cm thick.
4. Melt the remaining 1 tablespoon of butter in the microwave for 20 seconds. Using a pastry brush or your fingers, spread the melted butter onto the dough.
5. In a small bowl, mix together the brown sugar and cinnamon. Sprinkle the mixture across the surface of the dough. Roll the dough up, forming a long log. Using a pastry cutter or sharp knife, cut 10 cinnamon rolls.
6. Carefully place the cinnamon rolls into the air fryer basket. Then bake at 180°C/360°F for 6 minutes or until golden brown.
7. Meanwhile, in a small bowl, whisk together the powdered sugar and milk.
8. Plate the cinnamon rolls and drizzle the glaze over the surface before serving.

Variations & Ingredients Tips:

- Use different types of filling, such as cream cheese or fruit jam, for a variety of flavors.
- Add some chopped nuts or raisins to the filling for extra texture.
- For a vegan version, use non-dairy butter and milk in the dough and glaze.

Per Serving: Calories: 540; Total Fat: 20g; Saturated Fat: 12g; Cholesterol: 50mg; Sodium: 620mg; Total Carbs: 86g; Fiber: 2g; Sugars: 50g; Protein: 8g

Blueberry Muffins

Servings: 8 | Prep Time: 10 Minutes | Cooking Time: 14 Minutes

Ingredients:

- 1⅓ cups all-purpose flour
- ½ cup sugar
- 2 teaspoons baking powder
- ¼ teaspoon salt
- ⅓ cup canola oil
- 1 egg
- ½ cup milk
- ⅔ cup blueberries, fresh or frozen and thawed
- 8 foil muffin cups including paper liners

Directions:

1. Preheat air fryer to 165°C/330°F.
2. In a medium bowl, stir together flour, sugar, baking powder, and salt.
3. In a separate bowl, combine oil, egg, and milk and mix well.
4. Add egg mixture to dry ingredients and stir just until moistened.
5. Gently stir in blueberries.
6. Spoon batter evenly into muffin cups.
7. Place 4 muffin cups in air fryer basket and bake at 165°C/330°F for 14 minutes or until tops spring back when touched lightly.
8. Repeat previous step to cook remaining muffins.

Variations & Ingredients Tips:

- Use different berries like raspberries or blackberries.
- Add lemon or orange zest to the batter.
- Top with a streusel or crumb topping before baking.

Per Serving: Calories: 210; Total Fat: 9g; Saturated Fat: 1g; Cholesterol: 25mg; Sodium: 200mg; Total Carbs: 30g; Dietary Fiber: 1g; Total Sugars: 15g; Protein: 3g

Scones

Servings: 9 | Prep Time: 15 Minutes | Cooking Time: 8 Minutes Per Batch

Ingredients:

- 2 cups self-rising flour, plus ¼ cup for kneading
- ⅓ cup granulated sugar
- ¼ cup butter, cold
- 1 cup milk

Directions:

1. Preheat air fryer at 180°C/360°F.
2. In large bowl, stir together flour and sugar.
3. Cut cold butter into tiny cubes, and stir into flour mixture with fork.
4. Stir in milk until soft dough forms.
5. Sprinkle ¼ cup of flour onto wax paper and place dough on top. Knead lightly by folding and turning the dough about 6 to 8 times.
6. Pat dough into a 15 x 15 cm square.
7. Cut into 9 equal squares.
8. Place all squares in air fryer basket or as many as will fit in a single layer, close together but not touching.
9. Cook at 180°C/360°F for 8 minutes. When done, scones

will be lightly browned and spring back when pressed gently.
10. Repeat steps 8 and 9 to cook remaining scones.

Variations & Ingredients Tips:

- Add dried fruit, nuts or chocolate chips to the dough.
- Brush tops with milk or egg wash before baking for a glossy finish.
- Serve with jam, lemon curd or clotted cream.

Per Serving: Calories: 210; Total Fat: 7g; Saturated Fat: 4g; Cholesterol: 20mg; Sodium: 340mg; Total Carbs: 33g; Dietary Fiber: 1g; Total Sugars: 9g; Protein: 4g

Smooth Walnut-banana Loaf

Servings: 4 | Prep Time: 15 Minutes | Cooking Time: 40 Minutes

Ingredients:

- 1/3 cup peanut butter, melted
- 2 tbsp butter, melted and cooled
- ¾ cup flour
- ½ tsp salt
- ¼ tsp baking soda
- 2 ripe bananas
- 2 eggs
- 1 tsp lemon juice
- ½ cup evaporated cane sugar
- ½ cup ground walnuts
- 1 tbsp blackstrap molasses
- 1 tsp vanilla extract

Directions:

1. Preheat air fryer to 155°C/310°F.
2. Mix flour, salt, baking soda in one bowl.
3. In another bowl, mash bananas and eggs.
4. Stir in sugar, peanut butter, lemon, butter, walnuts, molasses and vanilla.
5. Fold in flour mixture just until combined.
6. Transfer to a parchment-lined baking dish.
7. Bake for 30-35 mins until a toothpick inserted in center comes out clean.

Variations & Ingredients Tips:

- Use almond or cashew butter instead of peanut.
- Add chocolate chips, coconut or chopped dates to the batter.
- Substitute some of the flour with oat or almond flour.

Per Serving: Calories: 535; Total Fat: 27g; Saturated Fat: 8g; Cholesterol: 103mg; Sodium: 489mg; Total Carbs: 66g; Dietary Fiber: 4g; Total Sugars: 39g; Protein: 12g

Pigs In A Blanket

Servings: 10 | Prep Time: 10 Minutes | Cooking Time: 8 Minutes

Ingredients:

- 1 cup all-purpose flour, plus more for rolling
- 1 tsp baking powder
- 1/4 cup salted butter, cut into pieces
- 1/2 cup buttermilk
- 10 fully cooked breakfast sausage links
- Egg wash (1 egg whisked with 2 tbsp water)
- Cooking spray

Directions:

1. In a bowl, whisk flour and baking powder. Cut in butter until crumbly.
2. Make a well, pour in buttermilk and mix into a dough.
3. On a floured surface, roll out dough to 1.3-cm thick.
4. Cut 10 rounds using a biscuit cutter.
5. Place a sausage link at the edge of each round and roll up, sealing edges.
6. Brush biscuits with egg wash and spray with cooking oil.
7. Place in air fryer basket spaced apart. Air fry at 170°C/340°F for 8 mins.

Variations & Ingredients Tips:

- Use puff pastry or crescent roll dough instead of biscuit dough.
- Add grated cheese or chopped herbs to the dough.
- Serve with mustard, maple syrup or hot sauce for dipping.

Per Serving: Calories: 180; Total Fat: 10g; Saturated Fat: 4g; Cholesterol: 20mg; Sodium: 400mg; Total Carbs: 17g; Dietary Fiber: 1g; Sugars: 1g; Protein: 5g

Broccoli Cornbread

Servings: 6 | Prep Time: 10 Minutes | Cooking Time: 18 Minutes

Ingredients:

- 1 cup frozen chopped broccoli, thawed and drained
- ¼ cup cottage cheese
- 1 egg, beaten
- 2 tablespoons minced onion
- 2 tablespoons melted butter
- ½ cup all-purpose flour
- ½ cup yellow cornmeal
- 1 teaspoon baking powder
- ½ teaspoon salt
- ¼ cup milk, plus 2 tablespoons
- Cooking spray

Directions:

1. Place thawed broccoli in colander and press with a spoon to squeeze out excess moisture.
2. Stir together all ingredients in a large bowl.
3. Spray 15x15cm baking pan with cooking spray.
4. Spread batter in pan and cook at 165°C/330°F for 18 minutes or until lightly browned and pulling away from sides.

Variations & Ingredients Tips:

- Add shredded cheddar cheese to the batter.
- Use fresh broccoli florets instead of frozen.
- Substitute greek yogurt for the cottage cheese.

Per Serving: Calories: 155; Total Fat: 6g; Saturated Fat: 3g; Cholesterol: 40mg; Sodium: 320mg; Total Carbs: 21g; Dietary Fiber: 2g; Total Sugars: 3g; Protein: 5g

Breakfast Pot Pies

Servings: 4 | Prep Time: 15 Minutes | Cooking Time: 20 Minutes

Ingredients:

- 1 refrigerated pie crust
- 227g pork breakfast sausage
- ¼ cup diced onion
- 1 garlic clove, minced
- ½ teaspoon ground black pepper
- ¼ teaspoon salt
- 1 cup chopped bell peppers
- 1 cup roasted potatoes
- 2 cups milk
- 2 to 3 tablespoons all-purpose flour

Directions:

1. Flatten pie crust and cut into 4 circles slightly larger than ramekins. Set aside.
2. Sauté sausage with onion, garlic, pepper and salt until browned. Add peppers and potatoes; cook 3-4 mins.
3. Portion sausage mixture equally into ramekins.
4. Make gravy: Boil milk, then simmer and whisk in 2-3 tbsp flour until thickened, about 5 mins.
5. Top sausage mixture with ½ cup gravy in each ramekin.
6. Place pie crust circles on top and crimp edges with a fork. Poke holes in top.
7. Air fry at 205°C/400°F for 6 mins until tops are golden brown.
8. Let cool 5 mins before serving.

Variations & Ingredients Tips:

- Use turkey or chicken sausage instead of pork.
- Substitute biscuit or crescent dough for the pie crust topping.
- Add shredded cheese to the gravy for extra richness.

Per Serving: Calories: 590; Total Fat: 35g; Saturated Fat: 13g; Cholesterol: 90mg; Sodium: 1130mg; Total Carbs: 46g; Dietary Fiber: 2g; Total Sugars: 7g; Protein: 21g

Ham & Cheese Sandwiches

Servings: 2 | Prep Time: 5 Minutes | Cooking Time: 15 Minutes

Ingredients:

- 5 g butter
- 4 bread slices
- 4 deli ham slices
- 4 Cheddar cheese slices
- 4 thick tomato slices
- 1 teaspoon dried oregano

Directions:

1. Preheat air fryer to 190°C/370°F. Smear 2 g of butter on only one side of each slice of bread and sprinkle with oregano. On one of the slices, layer 2 slices of ham, 2 slices of cheese, and 2 slices of tomato on the unbuttered side. Place the unbuttered side of another piece of bread onto the toppings. Place the sandwiches butter side down into the air fryer. Bake for 8 minutes, flipping once until crispy. Let cool slightly, cut in half and serve.

Variations & Ingredients Tips:

- Use turkey, roast beef or salami instead of ham.
- Swap cheddar for Swiss, provolone or pepper Jack cheese.
- Add some sliced avocado, pickles or roasted red peppers for extra flavor.

Per Serving: Calories: 477; Total Fat: 28g; Saturated Fat: 15g; Cholesterol: 97mg; Sodium: 1477mg; Total Carbs: 29g; Dietary Fiber: 2g; Total Sugars: 6g; Protein: 29g

Sugar-dusted Beignets

Servings: 4 | Prep Time: 20 Minutes | Cooking Time: 30 Minutes

Ingredients:

- 1 tsp fast active dry yeast
- 1/3 cup buttermilk
- 3 tbsp brown sugar
- 1 egg
- 1/2 tsp brandy
- 1 1/2 cups flour
- 3 tbsp chopped dried plums
- 3 tbsp golden raisins
- 2 tbsp butter, melted
- 2 tbsp powdered sugar

Directions:

1. Combine yeast with 3 tbsp water until frothy, 5 mins.
2. Add buttermilk, brown sugar, brandy, egg and stir.
3. Add flour and stir. Mix in plums and raisins.
4. Let rest 15 mins.
5. Preheat air fryer to 165°C/330°F.
6. Shape into 16 balls, drizzle with melted butter.
7. Air fry in batches for 5-8 mins until puffed and golden.
8. Toss in powdered sugar and serve.

Variations & Ingredients Tips:

- Use different dried fruits like apricots or cranberries.
- Add citrus zest or spices like cinnamon to the dough.
- Serve with chocolate, caramel or fruit dipping sauces.

Per Serving: Calories: 348; Total Fat: 8g; Saturated Fat: 5g; Cholesterol: 62mg; Sodium: 68mg; Total Carbs: 61g; Dietary Fiber: 2g; Total Sugars: 24g; Protein: 8g

Crispy Chicken Cakes

Servings: 4 | Prep Time: 10 Minutes | Cooking Time: 30 Minutes

Ingredients:

- 1 peeled Granny Smith apple, chopped
- 2 scallions, chopped
- 3 tablespoons ground almonds
- 1 teaspoon garlic powder
- 1 egg white
- 2 tablespoons apple juice
- Black pepper to taste
- 450 g ground chicken

Directions:

1. Preheat air fryer to 165°C/330°F.
2. Combine the apple, scallions, almonds, garlic powder, egg white, apple juice, and pepper in a bowl. Add the ground chicken using your hands. Mix well.
3. Make 8 patties and set four in the frying basket. Air Fry for 8-12 minutes until crispy. Repeat with the remaining patties.
4. Serve hot.

Variations & Ingredients Tips:

- Use different types of ground meat, such as turkey or pork, for a variety of flavors.
- Add some grated Parmesan cheese or bread crumbs to the patty mixture for extra flavor and texture.
- Serve the chicken cakes with a side of salsa or tzatziki sauce for dipping.

Per Serving: Calories: 240; Total Fat: 14g; Saturated Fat: 3.5g; Cholesterol: 115mg; Sodium: 120mg; Total Carbs: 6g; Fiber: 1g; Sugars: 4g; Protein: 26g

Baked Eggs With Bacon-tomato Sauce

Servings: 1 | Prep Time: 10 Minutes | Cooking Time: 12 Minutes

Ingredients:

- 1 teaspoon olive oil
- 2 tablespoons finely chopped onion
- 1 teaspoon chopped fresh oregano
- Pinch crushed red pepper flakes
- 1 (400g) can crushed or diced tomatoes
- Salt and freshly ground black pepper
- 2 slices bacon, chopped
- 2 large eggs
- ¼ cup grated Cheddar cheese
- Fresh parsley, chopped

Directions:

1. Make tomato sauce: Sauté onion, oregano and pepper flakes in oil for 5 mins. Add tomatoes, salt, pepper and simmer 10 mins.
2. Preheat air fryer to 205°C/400°F. Add a little water to drawer bottom.
3. Air fry bacon 5 mins until crispy. Drain grease from drawer.
4. Transfer sauce to a 18cm pie dish. Crack eggs over sauce and scatter bacon on top. Season with salt and pepper.
5. Air fry at 205°C/400°F for 5 mins until eggs are nearly set. Top with cheese and cook 2 more mins to melt.
6. Garnish with parsley and let cool slightly before serving.

Variations & Ingredients Tips:

- Use turkey or plant-based bacon.
- Add sautéed vegetables to the sauce.
- Substitute feta or goat cheese for the cheddar.

Per Serving: Calories: 335; Total Fat: 21g; Saturated Fat: 8g; Cholesterol: 330mg; Sodium: 630mg; Total Carbs: 18g; Dietary Fiber: 3g; Total Sugars: 8g; Protein: 20g

Sandwiches And Burgers Recipes

Philly Cheesesteak Sandwiches

Servings: 3 | Prep Time: 10 Minutes | Cooking Time: 9 Minutes

Ingredients:

- 340 grams Shaved beef
- 1 tablespoon Worcestershire sauce (gluten-free, if a concern)
- ¼ teaspoon Garlic powder
- ¼ teaspoon Mild paprika
- 6 tablespoons (45 grams) Frozen bell pepper strips (do not thaw)
- 2 slices, broken into rings Very thin yellow or white medium onion slice(s)
- 170 grams (6 to 8 slices) Provolone cheese slices
- 3 Long soft rolls such as hero, hoagie, or Italian sub rolls, or hot dog buns (gluten-free, if a concern), split open lengthwise

Directions:

1. Preheat the air fryer to 200°C/400°F.
2. When the machine is at temperature, spread the shaved beef in the basket, leaving a 1.25-cm perimeter around the meat for good air flow. Sprinkle the meat with the Worcestershire sauce, paprika, and garlic powder. Spread the peppers and onions on top of the meat.
3. Air-fry undisturbed for 6 minutes, or until cooked through. Set the cheese on top of the meat. Continue air-frying undisturbed for 3 minutes, or until the cheese has melted.
4. Use kitchen tongs to divide the meat and cheese layers in the basket between the rolls or buns. Serve hot.

Variations & Ingredients Tips:

- Use thinly sliced ribeye or sirloin steak instead of shaved beef for a more traditional texture.
- Add sliced mushrooms to the pepper and onion mixture for extra flavor and nutrition.
- Substitute provolone with American cheese or Cheez Whiz for a classic Philly taste.

Per Serving: Calories: 620; Cholesterol: 135mg; Total Fat: 32g; Saturated Fat: 15g; Sodium: 1320mg; Total Carbohydrates: 38g; Dietary Fiber: 2g; Total Sugars: 5g; Protein: 48g

Sausage And Pepper Heros

Servings: 3 | Prep Time: 10 Minutes | Cooking Time: 11 Minutes

Ingredients:

- 3 links (about 255 grams total) Sweet Italian sausages (gluten-free, if a concern)
- 1½ Medium red or green bell pepper(s), stemmed, cored, and cut into 1.25-cm-wide strips
- 1 medium Yellow or white onion(s), peeled, halved, and sliced into thin half-moons
- 3 Long soft rolls, such as hero, hoagie, or Italian sub rolls (gluten-free, if a concern), split open lengthwise
- For garnishing Balsamic vinegar
- For garnishing Fresh basil leaves

Directions:

1. Preheat the air fryer to 200°C/400°F.
2. When the machine is at temperature, set the sausage links in the basket in one layer and air-fry undisturbed for 5 minutes.
3. Add the pepper strips and onions. Continue air-frying, tossing and rearranging everything about once every minute, for 5 minutes, or until the sausages are browned and an instant-read meat thermometer inserted into one of the links registers 70°C/160°F.
4. Use a nonstick-safe spatula and kitchen tongs to transfer the sausages and vegetables to a cutting board. Set the rolls cut side down in the basket in one layer (working in batches as necessary) and air-fry undisturbed for 1 minute, to toast the rolls a bit and warm them up. Set 1 sausage with some pepper strips and onions in each warm roll, sprinkle balsamic vinegar over the sandwich fillings, and garnish with basil leaves.

Variations & Ingredients Tips:

- Use hot Italian sausage or chorizo for a spicier sandwich.
- Add sliced mushrooms or zucchini to the pepper and onion mixture for extra veggies.
- Top with shredded mozzarella or provolone cheese for a cheesy twist.

Per Serving (1 sandwich): Calories: 560; Cholesterol: 60mg; Total Fat: 36g; Saturated Fat: 12g; Sodium: 1420mg; Total Carbohydrates: 39g; Dietary Fiber: 3g; Total Sugars: 7g; Protein: 24g

Chili Cheese Dogs

Servings: 3 | Prep Time: 10 Minutes | Cooking Time: 12 Minutes

Ingredients:

- 340 grams Lean ground beef
- 1½ tablespoons Chile powder
- 240 grams plus 2 tablespoons Jarred sofrito
- 3 Hot dogs (gluten-free, if a concern)
- 3 Hot dog buns (gluten-free, if a concern), split open lengthwise
- 3 tablespoons Finely chopped scallion
- 60 grams Shredded Cheddar cheese

Directions:

1. Crumble the ground beef into a medium or large saucepan set over medium heat. Brown well, stirring often to break up the clumps. Add the chile powder and cook for 30 seconds, stirring the whole time. Stir in the sofrito and bring to a simmer. Reduce the heat to low and simmer, stirring occasionally, for 5 minutes. Keep warm.
2. Preheat the air fryer to 200°C/400°F.
3. When the machine is at temperature, put the hot dogs in the basket and air-fry undisturbed for 10 minutes, or until the hot dogs are bubbling and blistered, even a little crisp.
4. Use kitchen tongs to put the hot dogs in the buns. Top each with about 120 grams of the ground beef mixture, 1 tablespoon of the minced scallion, and 20 grams of the cheese. (The scallion should go under the cheese so it superheats and wilts a bit.) Set the filled hot dog buns in the basket and air-fry undisturbed for 2 minutes, or until the cheese has melted.
5. Remove the basket from the machine. Cool the chili cheese dogs in the basket for 5 minutes before serving.

Variations & Ingredients Tips:

- Use turkey or veggie hot dogs for a healthier option.
- Substitute cheddar cheese with your favorite melty cheese, such as pepper jack or Swiss.
- Add diced onions or jalapeños to the chili for extra flavor and heat.

Per Serving: Calories: 580; Cholesterol: 110mg; Total Fat: 32g; Saturated Fat: 13g; Sodium: 1420mg; Total Carbohydrates: 36g; Dietary Fiber: 5g; Total Sugars: 6g; Protein: 38g

Chicken Club Sandwiches

Servings: 3 | Prep Time: 15 Minutes | Cooking Time: 15 Minutes

Ingredients:

- 3 140- to 170-gram boneless skinless chicken breasts
- 6 Thick-cut bacon strips (gluten-free, if a concern)
- 3 Long soft rolls, such as hero, hoagie, or Italian sub rolls (gluten-free, if a concern)
- 3 tablespoons Regular, low-fat, or fat-free mayonnaise (gluten-free, if a concern)
- 3 Lettuce leaves, preferably romaine or iceberg
- 6 6-mm-thick tomato slices

Directions:

1. Preheat the air fryer to 190°C/375°F.
2. Wrap each chicken breast with 2 strips of bacon, spiraling the bacon around the meat, slightly overlapping the strips on each revolution. Start the second strip of bacon farther down the breast but on a line with the start of the first strip so they both end at a lined-up point on the chicken breast.
3. When the machine is at temperature, set the wrapped breasts bacon-seam side down in the basket with space between them. Air-fry undisturbed for 12 minutes, until the bacon is browned, crisp, and cooked through and an instant-read meat thermometer inserted into the center of a breast registers 75°C/165°F. You may need to add 2 minutes in the air fryer if the temperature is at 70°C/160°F.
4. Use kitchen tongs to transfer the breasts to a wire rack. Split the rolls open lengthwise and set them cut side down in the basket. Air-fry for 1 minute, or until warmed through.
5. Use kitchen tongs to transfer the rolls to a cutting board. Spread 1 tablespoon mayonnaise on the cut side of one half of each roll. Top with a chicken breast, lettuce leaf, and tomato slice. Serve warm.

Variations & Ingredients Tips:

- Use turkey bacon for a lower-fat option.
- Add sliced avocado or pickled onions for extra flavor and texture.
- Toast the rolls before assembling the sandwiches for a crispy texture.

Per Serving: Calories: 640; Cholesterol: 110mg; Total Fat: 34g; Saturated Fat: 9g; Sodium: 1180mg; Total Carbohydrates: 44g; Dietary Fiber: 2g; Total Sugars: 5g; Protein: 42g

Dijon Thyme Burgers

Servings: 3 | Prep Time: 15 Minutes | Cooking Time: 18 Minutes

Ingredients:

- 450 grams lean ground beef
- ⅓ cup panko breadcrumbs
- ¼ cup finely chopped onion
- 3 tablespoons Dijon mustard
- 1 tablespoon chopped fresh thyme
- 4 teaspoons Worcestershire sauce
- 1 teaspoon salt
- freshly ground black pepper
- Topping (optional):
- 2 tablespoons Dijon mustard
- 1 tablespoon dark brown sugar
- 1 teaspoon Worcestershire sauce
- 115 grams sliced Swiss cheese, optional

Directions:

1. Combine all the burger ingredients together in a large bowl and mix well. Divide the meat into 4 equal portions and then form the burgers, being careful not to over-handle the meat. One good way to do this is to throw the meat back and forth from one hand to another, packing the meat each time you catch it. Flatten the balls into patties, making an indentation in the center of each patty with your thumb (this will help it stay flat as it cooks) and flattening the sides of the burgers so that they will fit nicely into the air fryer basket.
2. Preheat the air fryer to 190°C/370°F.
3. If you don't have room for all four burgers, air-fry two or three burgers at a time for 8 minutes. Flip the burgers over and air-fry for another 6 minutes.
4. While the burgers are cooking combine the Dijon mustard, dark brown sugar, and Worcestershire sauce in a small bowl and mix well. This optional topping to the burgers really adds a boost of flavor at the end. Spread the Dijon topping evenly on each burger. If you cooked the burgers in batches, return the first batch to the cooker at this time – it's ok to place the fourth burger on top of the others in the center of the basket. Air-fry the burgers for another 3 minutes.
5. Finally, if desired, top each burger with a slice of Swiss cheese. Lower the air fryer temperature to 165°C/330°F and air-fry for another minute to melt the cheese. Serve the burgers on toasted brioche buns, dressed the way you like them.

Variations & Ingredients Tips:

- Use ground turkey or chicken for a leaner burger option.
- Add minced garlic or finely chopped herbs like parsley or chives for extra flavor.

- Substitute panko breadcrumbs with regular breadcrumbs or oats for a different texture.

Per Serving (1 burger with cheese): Calories: 500; Cholesterol: 120mg; Total Fat: 27g; Saturated Fat: 11g; Sodium: 1180mg; Total Carbohydrates: 21g; Dietary Fiber: 1g; Total Sugars: 5g; Protein: 41g

Lamb Burgers

Servings: 3 | Prep Time: 15 Minutes | Cooking Time: 17 Minutes

Ingredients:

- 510 grams Ground lamb
- 3 tablespoons Crumbled feta
- 1 teaspoon Minced garlic
- 1 teaspoon Tomato paste
- ¾ teaspoon Ground coriander
- ¾ teaspoon Ground dried ginger
- Up to ⅛ teaspoon Cayenne
- Up to a ⅛ teaspoon Table salt (optional)
- 3 Kaiser rolls or hamburger buns (gluten-free, if a concern), split open

Directions:

1. Preheat the air fryer to 190°C/375°F.
2. Gently mix the ground lamb, feta, garlic, tomato paste, coriander, ginger, cayenne, and salt (if using) in a bowl until well combined, trying to keep the bits of cheese intact. Form this mixture into two 15-cm patties for the small batch, three 12.5-cm patties for the medium, or four 12.5-cm patties for the large.
3. Set the patties in the basket in one layer and air-fry undisturbed for 16 minutes, or until an instant-read meat thermometer inserted into one burger registers 70°C/160°F. (The cheese is not an issue with the temperature probe in this recipe as it was for the Inside-Out Cheeseburgers, because the feta is so well mixed into the ground meat.)
4. Use a nonstick-safe spatula, and perhaps a flatware fork for balance, to transfer the burgers to a cutting board. Set the buns cut side down in the basket in one layer (working in batches as necessary) and air-fry undisturbed for 1 minute, to toast a bit and warm up. Serve the burgers warm in the buns.

Variations & Ingredients Tips:

- Substitute feta with goat cheese or crumbled blue cheese for a different flavor profile.
- Add finely chopped mint or parsley to the lamb mixture for a fresh, herbal taste.
- Serve with tzatziki sauce, sliced cucumbers, and red onions for a Greek-inspired burger.

Per Serving (1 burger): Calories: 560; Cholesterol: 140mg; Total Fat: 34g; Saturated Fat: 15g; Sodium: 580mg; Total Carbohydrates: 25g; Dietary Fiber: 1g; Total Sugars: 3g; Protein: 38g

Thanksgiving Turkey Sandwiches

Servings: 3 | Prep Time: 15 Minutes | Cooking Time: 10 Minutes

Ingredients:

- 1½ cups Herb-seasoned stuffing mix (not cornbread-style; gluten-free, if a concern)
- 1 Large egg white(s)
- 2 tablespoons Water
- 3 140- to 170-gram turkey breast cutlets
- Vegetable oil spray
- 4½ tablespoons Purchased cranberry sauce, preferably whole berry
- ⅛ teaspoon Ground cinnamon
- ⅛ teaspoon Ground dried ginger
- 4½ tablespoons Regular, low-fat, or fat-free mayonnaise (gluten-free, if a concern)
- 6 tablespoons Shredded Brussels sprouts
- 3 Kaiser rolls (gluten-free, if a concern), split open

Directions:

1. Preheat the air fryer to 190°C/375°F.
2. Put the stuffing mix in a heavy zip-closed bag, seal it, lay it flat on your counter, and roll a rolling pin over the bag to crush the stuffing mix to the consistency of rough sand. (Or you can pulse the stuffing mix to the desired consistency in a food processor.)
3. Set up and fill two shallow soup plates or small pie plates on your counter: one for the egg white(s), whisked with the water until foamy; and one for the ground stuffing mix.
4. Dip a cutlet in the egg white mixture, coating both sides and letting any excess egg white slip back into the rest. Set the cutlet in the ground stuffing mix and coat it evenly on both sides, pressing gently to coat well on both sides. Lightly coat the cutlet on both sides with vegetable oil spray, set it aside, and continue dipping and coating the remaining cutlets in the same way.
5. Set the cutlets in the basket and air-fry undisturbed for 10 minutes, or until crisp and brown. Use kitchen tongs to transfer the cutlets to a wire rack to cool for a few minutes.
6. Meanwhile, stir the cranberry sauce with the cinnamon and ginger in a small bowl. Mix the shredded Brussels sprouts and mayonnaise in a second bowl until the vegetable is evenly coated.
7. Build the sandwiches by spreading about 1½ tablespoons of the cranberry mixture on the cut side of the bottom half of each roll. Set a cutlet on top, then spread about 3 tablespoons of the Brussels sprouts mixture evenly over the cutlet. Set the other half of the roll on top and serve warm.

Variations & Ingredients Tips:

- Use leftover roasted turkey instead of turkey cutlets for a post-Thanksgiving sandwich.
- Substitute Brussels sprouts with shredded cabbage or kale for a different texture and flavor.
- Add a slice of brie or provolone cheese to the sandwich

for extra creaminess.

Per Serving: Calories: 530; Cholesterol: 75mg; Total Fat: 22g; Saturated Fat: 4g; Sodium: 1180mg; Total Carbohydrates: 53g; Dietary Fiber: 4g; Total Sugars: 15g; Protein: 33g

Chicken Apple Brie Melt

Servings: 3 | Prep Time: 10 Minutes | Cooking Time: 13 Minutes

Ingredients:

- 3 140 to 170-gram boneless skinless chicken breasts
- Vegetable oil spray
- 1½ teaspoons Dried herbes de Provence
- 85 grams Brie, rind removed, thinly sliced
- 6 Thin cored apple slices
- 3 French rolls (gluten-free, if a concern)
- 2 tablespoons Dijon mustard (gluten-free, if a concern)

Directions:

1. Preheat the air fryer to 190°C/375°F.
2. Lightly coat all sides of the chicken breasts with vegetable oil spray. Sprinkle the breasts evenly with the herbes de Provence.
3. When the machine is at temperature, set the breasts in the basket and air-fry undisturbed for 10 minutes.
4. Top the chicken breasts with the apple slices, then the cheese. Air-fry undisturbed for 2 minutes, or until the cheese is melty and bubbling.
5. Use a nonstick-safe spatula and kitchen tongs, for balance, to transfer the breasts to a cutting board. Set the rolls in the basket and air-fry for 1 minute to warm through. (Putting them in the machine without splitting them keeps the insides very soft while the outside gets a little crunchy.)
6. Transfer the rolls to the cutting board. Split them open lengthwise, then spread 1 teaspoon mustard on each cut side. Set a prepared chicken breast on the bottom of a roll and close with its top, repeating as necessary to make additional sandwiches. Serve warm.

Variations & Ingredients Tips:

- Substitute the Brie with Camembert or another soft cheese of your choice.
- Use pears instead of apples for a different flavor profile.
- Add baby spinach or arugula for extra greens and nutrition.

Per Serving: Calories: 510; Cholesterol: 135mg; Total Fat: 19g; Saturated Fat: 8g; Sodium: 670mg; Total Carbohydrates: 41g; Dietary Fiber: 2g; Total Sugars: 6g; Protein: 45g

Mexican Cheeseburgers

Servings: 4 | Prep Time: 20 Minutes | Cooking Time: 22 Minutes

Ingredients:

- 570 grams ground beef
- ¼ cup finely chopped onion
- ½ cup crushed yellow corn tortilla chips
- 1 (35-gram) packet taco seasoning
- ¼ cup canned diced green chilies
- 1 egg, lightly beaten
- 115 grams pepper jack cheese, grated
- 4 (30-cm) flour tortillas
- shredded lettuce, sour cream, guacamole, salsa (for topping)

Directions:

1. Combine the ground beef, minced onion, crushed tortilla chips, taco seasoning, green chilies, and egg in a large bowl. Mix thoroughly until combined – your hands are good tools for this. Divide the meat into four equal portions and shape each portion into an oval-shaped burger.
2. Preheat the air fryer to 190°C/370°F.
3. Air-fry the burgers for 18 minutes, turning them over halfway through the cooking time. Divide the cheese between the burgers, lower fryer to 170°C/340°F and air-fry for an additional 4 minutes to melt the cheese. (This will give you a burger that is medium-well. If you prefer your cheeseburger medium-rare, shorten the cooking time to about 15 minutes and then add the cheese and proceed with the recipe.)
4. While the burgers are cooking, warm the tortillas wrapped in aluminum foil in a 175°C/350°F oven, or in a skillet with a little oil over medium-high heat for a couple of minutes. Keep the tortillas warm until the burgers are ready.
5. To assemble the burgers, spread sour cream over three quarters of the tortillas and top each with some shredded lettuce and salsa. Place the Mexican cheeseburgers on the lettuce and top with guacamole. Fold the tortillas around the burger, starting with the bottom and then folding the sides in over the top. (A little sour cream can help hold the seam of the tortilla together.) Serve immediately.

Variations & Ingredients Tips:

- Use ground turkey or chicken for a leaner burger option.
- Substitute pepper jack cheese with Monterey Jack or cheddar cheese if preferred.
- Add sliced jalapeños or hot sauce to the burger mixture for extra heat.

Per Serving (1 burger): Calories: 780; Cholesterol: 165mg; Total Fat: 44g; Saturated Fat: 18g; Sodium: 1480mg; Total Carbohydrates: 51g; Dietary Fiber: 4g; Total Sugars: 4g; Protein: 46g

Asian Glazed Meatballs

Servings: 4 | Prep Time: 15 Minutes | Cooking Time: 10 Minutes

Ingredients:

- 1 large shallot, finely chopped
- 2 cloves garlic, minced
- 1 tablespoon grated fresh ginger
- 2 teaspoons fresh thyme, finely chopped
- 1½ cups brown mushrooms, very finely chopped (a food processor works well here)
- 2 tablespoons soy sauce
- freshly ground black pepper
- ½ kg ground beef
- ¼ kg ground pork
- 3 egg yolks
- 1 cup Thai sweet chili sauce (spring roll sauce)
- ¼ cup toasted sesame seeds
- 2 scallions, sliced

Directions:

1. Combine the shallot, garlic, ginger, thyme, mushrooms, soy sauce, freshly ground black pepper, ground beef and pork, and egg yolks in a bowl and mix the ingredients together. Gently shape the mixture into 24 balls, about the size of a golf ball.
2. Preheat the air fryer to 190°C/380°F.
3. Working in batches, air-fry the meatballs for 8 minutes, turning the meatballs over halfway through the cooking time. Drizzle some of the Thai sweet chili sauce on top of each meatball and return the basket to the air fryer, air-frying for another 2 minutes. Reserve the remaining Thai sweet chili sauce for serving.
4. As soon as the meatballs are done, sprinkle with toasted sesame seeds and transfer them to a serving platter. Scatter the scallions around and serve warm.

Variations & Ingredients Tips:

- Use a food processor to finely chop the mushrooms for better texture in the meatballs.
- Work in batches when air frying the meatballs to ensure even cooking and browning.
- Drizzle the Thai sweet chili sauce over the meatballs towards the end of cooking for a nice glaze.

Per Serving: Calories: 550; Cholesterol: 205mg; Total Fat: 32g; Saturated Fat: 11g; Sodium: 1300mg; Total Carbohydrates: 36g; Dietary Fiber: 2g; Total Sugars: 23g; Protein: 29g

Perfect Burgers

Servings: 3 | Prep Time: 10 Minutes | Cooking Time: 13 Minutes

Ingredients:

- 510 grams 90% lean ground beef
- 1½ tablespoons Worcestershire sauce (gluten-free, if a concern)
- ½ teaspoon Ground black pepper
- 3 Hamburger buns (gluten-free if a concern), split open

Directions:

1. Preheat the air fryer to 190°C/375°F.
2. Gently mix the ground beef, Worcestershire sauce, and pepper in a bowl until well combined but preserving as much of the meat's fibers as possible. Divide this mixture into two 15-cm patties for the small batch, three 12.5-cm patties for the medium, or four 12.5-cm patties for the large. Make a thumbprint indentation in the center of each patty, about halfway through the meat.
3. Set the patties in the basket in one layer with some space between them. Air-fry undisturbed for 10 minutes, or until an instant-read meat thermometer inserted into the center of a burger registers 70°C/160°F (a medium-well burger). You may need to add 2 minutes cooking time if the air fryer is at 180°C/360°F.
4. Use a nonstick-safe spatula, and perhaps a flatware fork for balance, to transfer the burgers to a cutting board. Set the buns cut side down in the basket in one layer (working in batches as necessary) and air-fry undisturbed for 1 minute, to toast a bit and warm up. Serve the burgers in the warm buns.

Variations & Ingredients Tips:

- Mix in finely chopped onions, garlic, or herbs to the burger mixture for extra flavor.
- Use a mixture of ground beef and ground pork or lamb for a juicier, more flavorful burger.
- Top burgers with your favorite cheese, bacon, avocado, or sautéed mushrooms.

Per Serving (1 burger): Calories: 420; Cholesterol: 105mg; Total Fat: 22g; Saturated Fat: 8g; Sodium: 460mg; Total Carbohydrates: 23g; Dietary Fiber: 1g; Total Sugars: 3g; Protein: 34g

Inside-out Cheeseburgers

Servings: 3 | Prep Time: 15 Minutes | Cooking Time: 9-11 Minutes

Ingredients:

- 510 grams 90% lean ground beef
- ¾ teaspoon Dried oregano
- ¾ teaspoon Table salt
- ¾ teaspoon Ground black pepper
- ¼ teaspoon Garlic powder
- 6 tablespoons (about 45 grams) Shredded Cheddar, Swiss, or other semi-firm cheese, or a purchased blend of shredded cheeses
- 3 Hamburger buns (gluten-free, if a concern), split open

Directions:

1. Preheat the air fryer to 190°C/375°F.
2. Gently mix the ground beef, oregano, salt, pepper, and garlic powder in a bowl until well combined without turning the mixture to mush. Form it into two 15-cm patties for the small batch, three for the medium, or four for the large.
3. Place 2 tablespoons of the shredded cheese in the center of each patty. With clean hands, fold the sides of the patty up

to cover the cheese, then pick it up and roll it gently into a ball to seal the cheese inside. Gently press it back into a 12.5-cm burger without letting any cheese squish out. Continue filling and preparing more burgers, as needed.
4. Place the burgers in the basket in one layer and air-fry undisturbed for 8 minutes for medium or 10 minutes for well-done. (An instant-read meat thermometer won't work for these burgers because it will hit the mostly melted cheese inside and offer a hotter temperature than the surrounding meat.)
5. Use a nonstick-safe spatula, and perhaps a flatware fork for balance, to transfer the burgers to a cutting board. Set the buns cut side down in the basket in one layer (working in batches as necessary) and air-fry undisturbed for 1 minute, to toast a bit and warm up. Cool the burgers a few minutes more, then serve them warm in the buns.

Variations & Ingredients Tips:

- Mix different types of cheese like cheddar, mozzarella, and blue cheese for a flavorful combination.
- Add finely chopped bacon or caramelized onions to the cheese stuffing for extra richness.
- Serve with your favorite burger toppings like lettuce, tomato, onion, and pickles.

Per Serving (1 burger): Calories: 480; Cholesterol: 125mg; Total Fat: 27g; Saturated Fat: 11g; Sodium: 720mg; Total Carbohydrates: 22g; Dietary Fiber: 1g; Total Sugars: 3g; Protein: 38g

Eggplant Parmesan Subs

Servings: 2 | Prep Time: 10 Minutes | Cooking Time: 13 Minutes

Ingredients:

- 4 Peeled eggplant slices (about 1.25 cm thick and 7.5 cm in diameter)
- Olive oil spray
- 2 tablespoons plus 2 teaspoons Jarred pizza sauce, any variety except creamy
- ¼ cup (about 20 grams) Finely grated Parmesan cheese
- 2 Small, long soft rolls, such as hero, hoagie, or Italian sub rolls (gluten-free, if a concern), split open lengthwise

Directions:

1. Preheat the air fryer to 175°C/350°F.
2. When the machine is at temperature, coat both sides of the eggplant slices with olive oil spray. Set them in the basket in one layer and air-fry undisturbed for 10 minutes, until lightly browned and softened.
3. Increase the machine's temperature to 190°C/375°F (or 185°C/370°F, if that's the closest setting—unless the machine is already at 180°C/360°F, in which case leave it alone). Top each eggplant slice with 2 teaspoons pizza sauce, then 1 tablespoon of cheese. Air-fry undisturbed for 2 minutes, or until the cheese has melted.
4. Use a nonstick-safe spatula, and perhaps a flatware fork for balance, to transfer the eggplant slices cheese side up to a cutting board. Set the roll(s) cut side down in the basket in one layer (working in batches as necessary) and air-fry undisturbed for 1 minute, to toast the rolls a bit and warm them up. Set 2 eggplant slices in each warm roll.

Variations & Ingredients Tips:

- Use zucchini slices instead of eggplant for a different vegetable option.
- Add a slice of fresh mozzarella on top of the Parmesan for extra cheesiness.
- Sprinkle some dried herbs like oregano or basil on the eggplant before cooking for extra flavor.

Per Serving (1 sandwich): Calories: 280; Cholesterol: 10mg; Total Fat: 9g; Saturated Fat: 3g; Sodium: 840mg; Total Carbohydrates: 40g; Dietary Fiber: 5g; Total Sugars: 8g; Protein: 11g

Salmon Burgers

Servings: 3 | Prep Time: 15 Minutes | Cooking Time: 8 Minutes

Ingredients:

- 510 grams Skinless salmon fillet, preferably fattier Atlantic salmon
- 1½ tablespoons Minced chives or the green part of a scallion
- ½ cup Plain panko bread crumbs (gluten-free, if a concern)
- 1½ teaspoons Dijon mustard (gluten-free, if a concern)
- 1½ teaspoons Drained and rinsed capers, minced
- 1½ teaspoons Lemon juice
- ¼ teaspoon Table salt
- ¼ teaspoon Ground black pepper
- Vegetable oil spray

Directions:

1. Preheat the air fryer to 190°C/375°F.
2. Cut the salmon into pieces that will fit in a food processor. Cover and pulse until coarsely chopped. Add the chives and pulse to combine, until the fish is ground but not a paste. Scrape down and remove the blade. Scrape the salmon mixture into a bowl. Add the bread crumbs, mustard, capers, lemon juice, salt, and pepper. Stir gently until well combined.
3. Use clean and dry hands to form the mixture into two 12.5-cm patties for a small batch, three 12.5-cm patties for a medium batch, or four 12.5-cm patties for a large one.
4. Coat both sides of each patty with vegetable oil spray. Set them in the basket in one layer and air-fry undisturbed for 8 minutes, or until browned and an instant-read meat thermometer inserted into the center of a burger registers 65°C/145°F.

5. Use a nonstick-safe spatula, and perhaps a flatware fork for balance, to transfer the burgers to a wire rack. Cool for 2 or 3 minutes before serving.

Variations & Ingredients Tips:

- Substitute salmon with canned or leftover cooked salmon for convenience.
- Add finely chopped red bell pepper or celery to the burger mixture for extra crunch and flavor.
- Serve on toasted buns with lettuce, tomato, and a dollop of tartar sauce or remoulade.

Per Serving (1 burger): Calories: 320; Cholesterol: 95mg; Total Fat: 16g; Saturated Fat: 3g; Sodium: 440mg; Total Carbohydrates: 15g; Dietary Fiber: 1g; Total Sugars: 1g; Protein: 31g

Thai-style Pork Sliders

Servings: 4 | Prep Time: 15 Minutes | Cooking Time: 15 Minutes

Ingredients:

- 310 grams Ground pork
- 2½ tablespoons Very thinly sliced scallions, white and green parts
- 4 teaspoons Minced peeled fresh ginger
- 2½ teaspoons Fish sauce (gluten-free, if a concern)
- 2 teaspoons Thai curry paste (see the headnote; gluten-free, if a concern)
- 2 teaspoons Light brown sugar
- ¾ teaspoon Ground black pepper
- 4 Slider buns (gluten-free, if a concern)

Directions:

1. Preheat the air fryer to 190°C/375°F.
2. Gently mix the pork, scallions, ginger, fish sauce, curry paste, brown sugar, and black pepper in a bowl until well combined. With clean, wet hands, form about 80 grams of the pork mixture into a slider about 6.5-cm in diameter. Repeat until you use up all the meat—3 sliders for the small batch, 4 for the medium, and 6 for the large. (Keep wetting your hands to help the patties adhere.)
3. When the machine is at temperature, set the sliders in the basket in one layer. Air-fry undisturbed for 14 minutes, or until the sliders are golden brown and caramelized at their edges and an instant-read meat thermometer inserted into the center of a slider registers 70°C/160°F.
4. Use a nonstick-safe spatula, and perhaps a flatware fork for balance, to transfer the sliders to a cutting board. Set the buns cut side down in the basket in one layer (working in batches as necessary) and air-fry undisturbed for 1 minute, to toast a bit and warm up. Serve the sliders warm in the buns.

Variations & Ingredients Tips:

- Use ground chicken or turkey for a leaner slider option.
- Substitute Thai curry paste with red curry paste or green curry paste for a different flavor profile.
- Serve with pickled vegetables, cilantro, and sriracha mayonnaise for extra Thai-inspired toppings.

Per Serving (1 slider): Calories: 240; Cholesterol: 65mg; Total Fat: 13g; Saturated Fat: 4g; Sodium: 490mg; Total Carbohydrates: 18g; Dietary Fiber: 1g; Total Sugars: 4g; Protein: 15g

Best-ever Roast Beef Sandwiches

Servings: 6 | Prep Time: 10 Minutes | Cooking Time: 30-50 Minutes

Ingredients:

- 2½ teaspoons Olive oil
- 1½ teaspoons Dried oregano
- 1½ teaspoons Dried thyme
- 1½ teaspoons Onion powder
- 1½ teaspoons Table salt
- 1½ teaspoons Ground black pepper
- 1 kg Beef eye of round
- 6 Round soft rolls, such as Kaiser rolls or hamburger buns (gluten-free, if a concern), split open lengthwise
- ¾ cup Regular, low-fat, or fat-free mayonnaise (gluten-free, if a concern)
- 6 Romaine lettuce leaves, rinsed
- 6 Round tomato slices (0.5 cm thick)

Directions:

1. Preheat the air fryer to 180°C/350°F.
2. Mix the oil, oregano, thyme, onion powder, salt, and pepper in a small bowl. Spread this mixture all over the eye of round.
3. When the machine is at temperature, set the beef in the basket and air-fry for 30 to 50 minutes (the range depends on the size of the cut), turning the meat twice, until an instant-read meat thermometer inserted into the thickest piece of the meat registers 55°C/130°F for rare, 60°C/140°F for medium, or 65°C/150°F for well-done.
4. Use kitchen tongs to transfer the beef to a cutting board. Cool for 10 minutes. If serving now, carve into 3-mm-thick slices. Spread each roll with 2 tablespoons mayonnaise and divide the beef slices between the rolls. Top with a lettuce leaf and a tomato slice and serve. Or set the beef in a container, cover, and refrigerate for up to 3 days to make cold roast beef sandwiches anytime.

Variations & Ingredients Tips:

- Experiment with different herbs and spices in the rub, such as garlic powder, paprika, or rosemary.
- Add sliced red onions or pickles for extra flavor and crunch.
- Use leftover roast beef for cold sandwiches or salads.

Per Serving: Calories: 560; Cholesterol: 115mg; Total Fat: 27g; Saturated Fat: 6g; Sodium: 980mg; Total Carbohydrates:

32g; Dietary Fiber: 2g; Total Sugars: 4g; Protein: 47g

Dietary Fiber: 8g; Total Sugars: 2g; Protein: 10g

Black Bean Veggie Burgers

Servings: 3 | Prep Time: 15 Minutes | Cooking Time: 10 Minutes

Ingredients:

- 1 cup Drained and rinsed canned black beans
- ⅓ cup Pecan pieces
- ⅓ cup Rolled oats (not quick-cooking or steel-cut; gluten-free, if a concern)
- 2 tablespoons (or 1 small egg) Pasteurized egg substitute, such as Egg Beaters (gluten-free, if a concern)
- 2 teaspoons Red ketchup-like chili sauce, such as Heinz
- ¼ teaspoon Ground cumin
- ¼ teaspoon Dried oregano
- ¼ teaspoon Table salt
- ¼ teaspoon Ground black pepper
- Olive oil
- Olive oil spray

Directions:

1. Preheat the air fryer to 200°C/400°F.
2. Put the beans, pecans, oats, egg substitute or egg, chili sauce, cumin, oregano, salt, and pepper in a food processor. Cover and process to a coarse paste that will hold its shape like sugar-cookie dough, adding olive oil in 1-teaspoon increments to get the mixture to blend smoothly. The amount of olive oil is actually dependent on the internal moisture content of the beans and the oats. Figure on about 1 tablespoon (three 1-teaspoon additions) for the smaller batch, with proportional increases for the other batches. A little too much olive oil can't hurt, but a dry paste will fall apart as it cooks and a far-too-wet paste will stick to the basket.
3. Scrape down and remove the blade. Using clean, wet hands, form the paste into two 10 cm patties for the small batch, three 10 cm patties for the medium, or four 10 cm patties for the large batch, setting them one by one on a cutting board. Generously coat both sides of the patties with olive oil spray.
4. Set them in the basket in one layer. Air-fry undisturbed for 10 minutes, or until lightly browned and crisp at the edges.
5. Use a nonstick-safe spatula, and perhaps a flatware fork for balance, to transfer the burgers to a wire rack. Cool for 5 minutes before serving.

Variations & Ingredients Tips:

- Add finely chopped vegetables like bell peppers, onions, or carrots for extra flavor and nutrition.
- Experiment with different spices and herbs, such as smoked paprika, garlic powder, or cilantro.
- For a gluten-free version, ensure all ingredients are certified gluten-free.

Per Serving: Calories: 280; Cholesterol: 0mg; Total Fat: 15g; Saturated Fat: 2g; Sodium: 420mg; Total Carbohydrates: 28g;

Inside Out Cheeseburgers

Servings: 2 | Prep Time: 15 Minutes | Cooking Time: 20 Minutes

Ingredients:

- 340 grams lean ground beef
- 3 tablespoons minced onion
- 4 teaspoons ketchup
- 2 teaspoons yellow mustard
- salt and freshly ground black pepper
- 4 slices of Cheddar cheese, broken into smaller pieces
- 8 hamburger dill pickle chips

Directions:

1. Combine the ground beef, minced onion, ketchup, mustard, salt and pepper in a large bowl. Mix well to thoroughly combine the ingredients. Divide the meat into four equal portions.
2. To make the stuffed burgers, flatten each portion of meat into a thin patty. Place 4 pickle chips and half of the cheese onto the center of two of the patties, leaving a rim around the edge of the patty exposed. Place the remaining two patties on top of the first and press the meat together firmly, sealing the edges tightly. With the burgers on a flat surface, press the sides of the burger with the palm of your hand to create a straight edge. This will help keep the stuffing inside the burger while it cooks.
3. Preheat the air fryer to 190°C/370°F.
4. Place the burgers inside the air fryer basket and air-fry for 20 minutes, flipping the burgers over halfway through the cooking time.
5. Serve the cheeseburgers on buns with lettuce and tomato.

Variations & Ingredients Tips:

- Use different types of cheese like Swiss, pepper jack, or blue cheese for a unique flavor.
- Add crispy bacon pieces or sautéed mushrooms to the stuffing for extra richness.
- Brush the burgers with a mixture of melted butter and minced garlic before cooking for added flavor.

Per Serving (1 burger): Calories: 510; Cholesterol: 145mg; Total Fat: 32g; Saturated Fat: 14g; Sodium: 780mg; Total Carbohydrates: 12g; Dietary Fiber: 1g; Total Sugars: 6g; Protein: 42g

Crunchy Falafel Balls

Servings: 8 | Prep Time: 15 Minutes | Cooking Time: 16 Minutes

Ingredients:

- 600 grams Drained and rinsed canned chickpeas
- 60 grams Olive oil
- 3 tablespoons All-purpose flour
- 1½ teaspoons Dried oregano
- 1½ teaspoons Dried sage leaves
- 1½ teaspoons Dried thyme
- ¾ teaspoon Table salt
- Olive oil spray

Directions:

1. Preheat the air fryer to 200°C/400°F.
2. Place the chickpeas, olive oil, flour, oregano, sage, thyme, and salt in a food processor. Cover and process into a paste, stopping the machine at least once to scrape down the inside of the canister.
3. Scrape down and remove the blade. Using clean, wet hands, form 2 tablespoons of the paste into a ball, then continue making 9 more balls for a small batch, 15 more for a medium one, and 19 more for a large batch. Generously coat the balls in olive oil spray.
4. Set the balls in the basket in one layer with a little space between them and air-fry undisturbed for 16 minutes, or until well browned and crisp.
5. Dump the contents of the basket onto a wire rack. Cool for 5 minutes before serving.

Variations & Ingredients Tips:

- Add minced garlic, onion, or herbs like parsley or cilantro for extra flavor.
- Serve with tahini sauce, hummus, or tzatziki for dipping.
- Make a falafel sandwich by stuffing pita bread with falafel balls, lettuce, tomato, and sauce.

Per Serving (2 falafel balls): Calories: 170; Cholesterol: 0mg; Total Fat: 9g; Saturated Fat: 1g; Sodium: 230mg; Total Carbohydrates: 18g; Dietary Fiber: 4g; Total Sugars: 2g; Protein: 5g

Reuben Sandwiches

Servings: 2 | Prep Time: 10 Minutes | Cooking Time: 11 Minutes

Ingredients:

- 225 grams Sliced deli corned beef
- 4 teaspoons Regular or low-fat mayonnaise (not fat-free)
- 4 Rye bread slices
- 2 tablespoons plus 2 teaspoons Russian dressing
- ½ cup Purchased sauerkraut, squeezed by the handful over the sink to get rid of excess moisture
- 55 grams (2 to 4 slices) Swiss cheese slices (optional)

Directions:

1. Set the corned beef in the basket, slip the basket into the machine, and heat the air fryer to 200°C/400°F. Air-fry undisturbed for 3 minutes from the time the basket is put in the machine, just to warm up the meat.
2. Use kitchen tongs to transfer the corned beef to a cutting board. Spread 1 teaspoon mayonnaise on one side of each slice of rye bread, rubbing the mayonnaise into the bread with a small flatware knife.
3. Place the bread slices mayonnaise side down on a cutting board. Spread the Russian dressing over the "dry" side of each slice. For one sandwich, top one slice of bread with the corned beef, sauerkraut, and cheese (if using). For two sandwiches, top two slices of bread each with half of the corned beef, sauerkraut, and cheese (if using). Close the sandwiches with the remaining bread, setting it mayonnaise side up on top.
4. Set the sandwich(es) in the basket and air-fry undisturbed for 8 minutes, or until browned and crunchy.
5. Use a nonstick-safe spatula, and perhaps a flatware fork for balance, to transfer the sandwich(es) to a cutting board. Cool for 2 or 3 minutes before slicing in half and serving.

Variations & Ingredients Tips:

- Substitute corned beef with pastrami for a classic New York deli taste.
- Use Thousand Island dressing instead of Russian dressing for a tangy, sweet flavor.
- Add sliced dill pickles or mustard to the sandwich for extra zing.

Per Serving (1 sandwich): Calories: 520; Cholesterol: 75mg; Total Fat: 30g; Saturated Fat: 9g; Sodium: 2020mg; Total Carbohydrates: 36g; Dietary Fiber: 4g; Total Sugars: 6g; Protein: 29g

Appetizers And Snacks

Crispy Ravioli Bites

Servings: 5 | Prep Time: 15 Minutes | Cooking Time: 7 Minutes

Ingredients:

- ⅓ cup All-purpose flour
- 1 Large egg(s), well beaten
- ⅔ cup Seasoned Italian-style dried bread crumbs
- 285 g Frozen mini ravioli, meat or cheese, thawed
- Olive oil spray

Directions:

1. Preheat the air fryer to 200°C/400°F.
2. Pour the flour into a medium bowl. Set up and fill two shallow soup plates or small pie plates on your counter: one with the beaten egg(s) and one with the bread crumbs.
3. Pour all the ravioli into the flour and toss well to coat. Pick up 1 ravioli, gently shake off any excess flour, and dip the ravioli in the egg(s), coating both sides. Let any excess egg slip back into the rest, then set the ravioli in the bread crumbs, turning it several times until lightly and evenly coated on all sides. Set aside on a cutting board and continue on with the remaining ravioli.
4. Lightly coat the ravioli on both sides with olive oil spray, then set them in the basket in as close to a single layer as you can. Some can lean up against the side of the basket. Air-fry for 7 minutes, tossing the basket at the 4-minute mark to rearrange the pieces, until brown and crisp.
5. Pour the contents of the basket onto a wire rack. Cool for 5 minutes before serving.

Variations & Ingredients Tips:

- Use wonton wrappers filled with your favorite ingredients instead of ravioli.
- Sprinkle the cooked ravioli with grated Parmesan cheese or chopped fresh herbs.
- Serve with marinara sauce or pesto for dipping.

Per Serving: Calories: 216; Total Fat: 6g; Saturated Fat: 1g; Cholesterol: 41mg; Sodium: 503mg; Total Carbs: 32g; Dietary Fiber: 2g; Total Sugars: 2g; Protein: 9g

Crab Rangoon

Servings: 18 | Prep Time: 20 Minutes | Cooking Time: 6 Minutes

Ingredients:

- 115 g Crabmeat, preferably backfin or claw, picked over for shells and cartilage
- 45 g Regular or low-fat cream cheese (not fat-free), softened to room temperature
- 1½ tablespoons Minced scallion
- 1½ teaspoons Minced garlic
- 1½ teaspoons Worcestershire sauce
- 18 Wonton wrappers (thawed, if necessary)
- Vegetable oil spray

Directions:

1. Preheat the air fryer to 200°C/400°F.
2. Gently stir the crab, cream cheese, scallion, garlic, and Worcestershire sauce in a medium bowl until well combined.
3. Set a bowl of water on a clean, dry work surface or next to a large cutting board. Set one wonton wrapper on the surface, then put a teaspoonful of the crab mixture in the center of the wrapper. Dip your clean finger in the water and run it around the edge of the wrapper. Bring all four sides up to the center and over the filling, and pinch them together in the middle to seal without covering all of the filling. The traditional look is for the corners of the filled wonton to become four open "flower petals" radiating out from the filled center. Set the filled wonton aside and continue making more as needed. (If you want a video tutorial on filling these, see ours at our YouTube channel, Cooking with Bruce and Mark.)
4. Generously coat the filled wontons with vegetable oil spray. Set them sealed side up in the basket with a little room among them. Air-fry undisturbed for 6 minutes, or until golden brown and crisp.
5. Use a nonstick-safe spatula to gently transfer the wontons to a wire rack. Cool for 5 minutes before serving warm.

Variations & Ingredients Tips:

- Use imitation crab meat, cooked shrimp or smoked salmon instead of crab.
- Add some sriracha, sambal oelek or sweet chili sauce to the filling.
- Serve with soy sauce, duck sauce or spicy mustard for dipping.

Per Serving: Calories: 49; Total Fat: 2g; Saturated Fat: 1g; Cholesterol: 11mg; Sodium: 91mg; Total Carbs: 5g; Dietary Fiber: 0g; Total Sugars: 0g; Protein: 2g

Crabby Fries

Servings: 2 | Prep Time: 15 Minutes | Cooking Time: 30 Minutes

Ingredients:

- 2 to 3 large russet potatoes, peeled and cut into 13 mm sticks
- 2 tablespoons vegetable oil
- 2 tablespoons butter
- 2 tablespoons flour
- 1 to 1½ cups milk
- ½ cup grated white Cheddar cheese
- pinch of nutmeg
- ½ teaspoon salt
- freshly ground black pepper
- 1 tablespoon Old Bay® Seasoning

Directions:

1. Bring a large saucepan of salted water to a boil on the stovetop while you peel and cut the potatoes. Blanch the potatoes in the boiling salted water for 4 minutes while you Preheat the air fryer to 200°C/400°F. Strain the potatoes and rinse them with cold water. Dry them well with a clean kitchen towel.

2. Toss the dried potato sticks gently with the oil and place them in the air fryer basket. Air-fry for 25 minutes, shaking the basket a few times while the fries cook to help them brown evenly.
3. While the fries are cooking, melt the butter in a medium saucepan. Whisk in the flour and cook for one minute. Slowly add 1 cup of milk, whisking constantly. Bring the mixture to a simmer and continue to whisk until it thickens. Remove the pan from the heat and stir in the Cheddar cheese. Add a pinch of nutmeg and season with salt and freshly ground black pepper. Transfer the warm cheese sauce to a serving dish. Thin with more milk if you want the sauce a little thinner.
4. As soon as the French fries have finished air-frying transfer them to a large bowl and season them with the Old Bay® Seasoning. Return the fries to the air fryer basket and air-fry for an additional 3 to 5 minutes. Serve immediately with the warm white Cheddar cheese sauce.

Variations & Ingredients Tips:

- Use sweet potatoes or parsnips instead of russets.
- Add some cooked crabmeat or shrimp to the cheese sauce.
- Sprinkle the fries with chopped parsley, chives or bacon bits before serving.

Per Serving: Calories: 702; Total Fat: 43g; Saturated Fat: 17g; Cholesterol: 62mg; Sodium: 1614mg; Total Carbs: 63g; Dietary Fiber: 5g; Total Sugars: 6g; Protein: 17g

Savory Sausage Balls

Servings: 10 | Prep Time: 15 Minutes | Cooking Time: 8 Minutes

Ingredients:

- 2 cups all-purpose flour
- 1 tablespoon baking powder
- 1/2 teaspoon garlic powder
- 1/4 teaspoon onion powder
- 1/2 teaspoon salt
- 3 tablespoons milk
- 2 1/2 cups grated pepper jack cheese
- 450-g fresh sausage, casing removed

Directions:

1. Preheat the air fryer to 370°F/188°C. In a large bowl, whisk together the flour, baking powder, garlic powder, onion powder, and salt. Add in the milk, grated cheese, and sausage. Using a tablespoon, scoop out the sausage and roll it between your hands to form rounded balls. You should get around 32 balls. Place them in the air fryer basket in a single layer, working in batches. Cook for 8 minutes, or until the outer coating turns light brown. Carefully remove, repeating with remaining sausage balls.

Variations & Ingredients Tips:

- Use spicy or Italian sausage for a kick of flavor.
- Roll in breadcrumbs before air frying for extra crunch.
- Serve with ranch, honey mustard or marinara for dipping.

Per Serving: Calories: 293; Total Fat: 20g; Saturated Fat: 9g; Cholesterol: 49mg; Sodium: 613mg; Total Carbs: 16g; Dietary Fiber: 1g; Total Sugars: 1g; Protein: 13g

Tomato & Basil Bruschetta

Servings: 4 | Prep Time: 10 Minutes | Cooking Time: 15 Minutes

Ingredients:

- 3 red tomatoes, diced
- ½ ciabatta loaf
- 1 garlic clove, minced
- 1 fresh mozzarella ball, sliced
- 1 tbsp olive oil
- 10 fresh basil, chopped
- 1 tsp balsamic vinegar
- Pinch of salt

Directions:

1. Preheat air fryer to 190°C/370°F. Mix tomatoes, olive oil, salt, vinegar, basil, and garlic in a bowl until well combined. Cut the loaf into 6 slices, about 2.5-cm thick. Spoon the tomato mixture over the bread and top with one mozzarella slice. Repeat for all bruschettas. Put the bruschettas in the foil-lined frying basket and bake for 5 minutes until golden. Serve.

Variations & Ingredients Tips:

- Add a drizzle of pesto or balsamic glaze over the bruschetta for extra flavor.
- Use goat cheese, ricotta, or burrata instead of mozzarella for a creamier topping.
- Grill the bread slices before topping for a smoky, charred taste.

Per Serving: Calories: 237; Total Fat: 11g; Saturated Fat: 4g; Cholesterol: 22mg; Sodium: 362mg; Total Carbohydrates: 26g; Dietary Fiber: 2g; Total Sugars: 4g; Protein: 10g

Bacon & Blue Cheese Tartlets

Servings: 6 | Prep Time: 15 Minutes | Cooking Time: 30 Minutes

Ingredients:

- 6 bacon slices
- 16 phyllo tartlet shells
- ½ cup diced blue cheese
- 3 tbsp apple jelly

Directions:

1. Preheat the air fryer to 200°C/400°F. Put the bacon in a single layer in the frying basket and Air Fry for 14 minutes, turning once halfway through. Remove and drain on paper towels, then crumble when cool. Wipe the fryer clean. Fill the tartlet shells with bacon and the blue cheese cubes

and add a dab of apple jelly on top of the filling. Lower the temperature to 175°C/350°F, then put the shells in the frying basket. Air Fry until the cheese melts and the shells brown, about 5-6 minutes. Remove and serve.

Variations & Ingredients Tips:

- Use goat cheese or brie instead of blue cheese.
- Top with a slice of fresh pear or apple instead of jelly.
- Garnish with chopped chives or thyme leaves.

Per Serving: Calories: 128; Total Fat: 8g; Saturated Fat: 3g; Cholesterol: 14mg; Sodium: 286mg; Total Carbs: 9g; Dietary Fiber: 0g; Total Sugars: 4g; Protein: 5g

Nicoise Deviled Eggs

Servings: 4 | Prep Time: 10 Minutes | Cooking Time: 20 Minutes

Ingredients:

- 4 eggs
- 2 tbsp mayonnaise
- 10 chopped Nicoise olives
- 2 tbsp goat cheese crumbles
- Salt and pepper to taste
- 2 tbsp chopped parsley

Directions:

1. Preheat air fryer to 130°C/260°F. Place the eggs in silicone muffin cups to avoid bumping around and cracking during the cooking process. Add silicone cups to the frying basket and air fry for 15 minutes. Remove and run the eggs under cold water. When cool, remove the shells and halve them lengthwise. Spoon yolks into a separate medium bowl and arrange white halves on a large plate. Mash the yolks with a fork. Stir in the remaining ingredients. Spoon mixture into white halves and scatter with mint to serve.

Variations & Ingredients Tips:

- Substitute Kalamata olives for Nicoise olives for a different briny flavor.
- Try using feta cheese instead of goat cheese for a saltier taste.
- Add a dash of hot sauce or Dijon mustard to the yolk mixture for extra zing.

Per Serving: Calories: 124; Total Fat: 10g; Saturated Fat: 3g; Cholesterol: 191mg; Sodium: 236mg; Total Carbs: 1g; Dietary Fiber: 0g; Total Sugars: 0g; Protein: 7g

Chili Black Bean Empanadas

Servings: 4 | Prep Time: 10 Minutes | Cooking Time: 20 Minutes

Ingredients:

- ½ cup cooked black beans
- ¼ cup white onions, diced
- 1 tsp red chili powder
- ½ tsp paprika
- ½ tsp garlic salt
- ½ tsp ground cumin
- ½ tsp ground cinnamon
- 4 empanada dough shells

Directions:

1. Preheat air fryer to 175°C/350°F. Stir-fry black beans and onions in a pan over medium heat for 5 minutes. Add chili, paprika, garlic salt, cumin, and cinnamon. Set aside covered when onions are soft and the beans are hot.
2. On a clean workspace, lay the empanada shells. Spoon bean mixture onto shells without spilling. Fold the shells over to cover fully. Seal the edges with water and press with a fork. Transfer the empanadas to the foil-lined frying basket and Bake for 15 minutes, flipping once halfway through cooking. Cook until golden. Serve.

Variations & Ingredients Tips:

- Use refried pinto beans or black-eyed peas instead of black beans.
- Add some chopped jalapeños or hot sauce to the filling for extra spice.
- Serve with salsa, guacamole or sour cream for dipping.

Per Serving: Calories: 197, Cholesterol: 18mg, Total Fat: 8g, Saturated Fat: 3g, Sodium: 480mg, Total Carbohydrates: 27g, Dietary Fiber: 3g, Total Sugars: 2g, Protein: 5g

Turkey Spring Rolls

Servings: 4 | Prep Time: 20 Minutes | Cooking Time: 20 Minutes

Ingredients:

- 450 g turkey breast, grilled, cut into chunks
- 1 celery stalk, julienned
- 1 carrot, grated
- 1 tsp fresh ginger, minced
- 1 tsp sugar
- 1 tsp chicken stock powder
- 1 egg
- 1 tsp corn starch
- 6 spring roll wrappers

Directions:

1. Preheat the air fryer to 180°C/360°F. Mix the turkey, celery, carrot, ginger, sugar, and chicken stock powder in a large bowl. Combine thoroughly and set aside. In another bowl, beat the egg, and stir in the cornstarch. On a clean surface, spoon the turkey filling into each spring roll, roll up and seal the seams with the egg-cornstarch mixture. Put each roll in the greased frying basket and air fry for 7-8 minutes, flipping once until golden brown. Serve hot.

Variations & Ingredients Tips:

- Use cooked shrimp, pork, or tofu instead of turkey for a different protein.
- Add shredded cabbage, bean sprouts, or rice noodles to the filling for extra crunch and texture.
- Serve with hoisin sauce, peanut sauce, or soy sauce for

dipping.

Per Serving: Calories: 277; Total Fat: 4g; Saturated Fat: 1g; Cholesterol: 128mg; Sodium: 377mg; Total Carbohydrates: 21g; Dietary Fiber: 1g; Total Sugars: 2g; Protein: 37g

Cocktail Beef Bites

Servings: 4 | Prep Time: 15 Minutes | Cooking Time: 30 Minutes

Ingredients:

- 450 g sirloin tip, cubed
- 1 cup cheese pasta sauce
- 1 ½ cups soft bread crumbs
- 2 tbsp olive oil
- ½ tsp garlic powder
- ½ tsp dried thyme

Directions:

1. Preheat air fryer to 180°C/360°F. Toss the beef and the pasta sauce in a medium bowl. Set aside. In a shallow bowl, mix bread crumbs, oil, garlic, and thyme until well combined. Drop the cubes in the crumb mixture to coat. Place them in the greased frying basket and Bake for 6-8 minutes, shaking once until the beef is crisp and browned. Serve warm with cocktail forks or toothpicks.

Variations & Ingredients Tips:

- Use pork tenderloin or chicken breast instead of beef.
- Toss the cooked bites in buffalo sauce or BBQ sauce for extra flavor.
- Serve with ranch dressing or blue cheese dip on the side.

Per Serving: Calories: 456; Total Fat: 22g; Saturated Fat: 6g; Cholesterol: 89mg; Sodium: 670mg; Total Carbs: 32g; Dietary Fiber: 2g; Total Sugars: 3g; Protein: 34g

Rosemary Garlic Goat Cheese

Servings: 4 | Prep Time: 10 Minutes | Cooking Time: 20 Minutes

Ingredients:

- 2 peeled garlic cloves roasted
- 340 g goat cheese
- ½ cup grated Parmesan
- 1 egg, beaten
- 1 tbsp olive oil
- 1 tbsp apple cider vinegar
- Salt and pepper to taste
- 1 tsp chopped rosemary

Directions:

1. Preheat air fryer to 175°C/350°F. Carefully squeeze the garlic into a bowl and mash it with a fork until a paste is formed. Stir in goat cheese, Parmesan, egg, olive oil, vinegar, salt, black pepper, and rosemary. Spoon the mixture into a baking dish, and place the dish in the frying basket. Air fry for 7 minutes. Serve warm.

Variations & Ingredients Tips:

- Use different herbs like thyme, basil, or oregano instead of rosemary.
- Add sun-dried tomatoes, olives, or roasted red peppers for a Mediterranean twist.
- Serve with crostini, crackers, or sliced baguette for spreading.

Per Serving: Calories: 273; Total Fat: 22g; Saturated Fat: 13g; Cholesterol: 78mg; Sodium: 441mg; Total Carbs: 2g; Dietary Fiber: 0g; Total Sugars: 1g; Protein: 17g

Fried Brie With Cherry Tomatoes

Servings: 8 | Prep Time: 10 Minutes | Cooking Time: 15 Minutes

Ingredients:

- 1 baguette*
- 2 pints red and yellow cherry tomatoes
- 1 tablespoon olive oil
- salt and freshly ground black pepper
- 1 teaspoon balsamic vinegar
- 1 tablespoon chopped fresh parsley
- 1 (225 g) wheel of Brie cheese
- olive oil
- ½ teaspoon Italian seasoning (optional)
- 1 tablespoon chopped fresh basil

Directions:

1. Preheat the air fryer to 175°C/350°F.
2. Start by making the crostini. Slice the baguette diagonally into 13 mm slices and brush the slices with olive oil on both sides. Air-fry the baguette slices at 175°C/350°F in batches for 6 minutes or until lightly browned on all sides. Set the bread aside on your serving platter.
3. Toss the cherry tomatoes in a bowl with the olive oil, salt and pepper. Air-fry the cherry tomatoes for 3 to 5 minutes, shaking the basket a few times during the cooking process. The tomatoes should be soft and some of them will burst open. Toss the warm tomatoes with the balsamic vinegar and fresh parsley and set aside.
4. Cut a circle of parchment paper the same size as your wheel of Brie cheese. Brush both sides of the Brie wheel with olive oil and sprinkle with Italian seasoning, if using. Place the circle of parchment paper on one side of the Brie and transfer the Brie to the air fryer basket, parchment side down. Air-fry at 175°C/350°F for 8 to 10 minutes, or until the Brie is slightly puffed and soft to the touch.
5. Watch carefully and remove the Brie before the rind cracks and the cheese starts to leak out. Transfer the wheel to your serving platter and top with the roasted tomatoes. Sprinkle with basil and serve with the toasted bread slices.

Variations & Ingredients Tips:

- Use camembert or goat cheese instead of brie for a

different flavor.
- Top the cheese with caramelized onions, honey or fig jam.
- Serve with sliced apples, pears or grapes on the side.

Per Serving: Calories: 264; Total Fat: 14g; Saturated Fat: 8g; Cholesterol: 44mg; Sodium: 430mg; Total Carbs: 24g; Dietary Fiber: 2g; Total Sugars: 3g; Protein: 12g

Individual Pizzas

Servings: 2 | Prep Time: 10 Minutes | Cooking Time: 7 Minutes

Ingredients:

- 170 g Purchased fresh pizza dough (not a pre-baked crust)
- Olive oil spray
- 4½ tablespoons Purchased pizza sauce or purchased pesto
- ½ cup (about 60 g) Shredded semi-firm mozzarella

Directions:

1. Preheat the air fryer to 200°C/400°F.
2. Press the pizza dough into a 13 cm circle for a small air fryer, a 15 cm circle for a medium air fryer, or an 18 cm circle for a large machine. Generously coat the top of the dough with olive oil spray.
3. Remove the basket from the machine and set the dough oil side down in the basket. Smear the sauce or pesto over the dough, then sprinkle with the cheese.
4. Return the basket to the machine and air-fry undisturbed for 7 minutes, or until the dough is puffed and browned and the cheese has melted. (Extra toppings will not increase the cooking time, provided you add no extra cheese.)
5. Remove the basket from the machine and cool the pizza in it for 5 minutes. Use a large nonstick-safe spatula to transfer the pizza from the basket to a wire rack. Cool for 5 minutes more before serving.

Variations & Ingredients Tips:

- Use different sauces like Alfredo, BBQ or garlic oil.
- Add your favorite toppings like pepperoni, sausage, mushrooms or olives.
- Sprinkle with Parmesan cheese, red pepper flakes or fresh herbs after cooking.

Per Serving: Calories: 307; Total Fat: 12g; Saturated Fat: 5g; Cholesterol: 27mg; Sodium: 634mg; Total Carbs: 37g; Dietary Fiber: 2g; Total Sugars: 3g; Protein: 13g

Thai-style Crab Wontons

Servings: 4 | Prep Time: 20 Minutes | Cooking Time: 20 Minutes

Ingredients:

- 115 g cottage cheese, softened
- 70 g lump crabmeat
- 2 scallions, chopped
- 2 garlic cloves, minced
- 2 tsp tamari sauce
- 12 wonton wrappers
- 1 egg white, beaten
- 5 tbsp Thai sweet chili sauce

Directions:

1. Using a fork, mix together cottage cheese, crabmeat, scallions, garlic, and tamari sauce in a bowl. Set it near your workspace along with a small bowl of water. Place one wonton wrapper on a clean surface. The points should be facing so that it looks like a diamond. Put 1 level tbsp of the crab and cheese mix onto the center of the wonton wrapper. Dip your finger into the water and run the moist finger along the edges of the wrapper. Fold one corner of the wrapper to the opposite side and make a triangle. From the center out, press out any air and seal the edges. Continue this process until all of the wontons have been filled and sealed. Brush both sides of the wontons with beaten egg white. Preheat air fryer to 170°C/340°F. Place the wontons on the bottom of the greased frying basket in a single layer. Bake for 8 minutes, flipping the wontons once until golden brown and crispy. Serve hot and enjoy!

Variations & Ingredients Tips:

- Substitute crab with cooked, shredded chicken, pork, or shrimp for a different filling.
- Add finely chopped water chestnuts, bamboo shoots, or mushrooms for extra crunch and flavor.
- Serve with hoisin sauce, soy sauce, or plum sauce for dipping.

Per Serving: Calories: 204; Total Fat: 4g; Saturated Fat: 1g; Cholesterol: 37mg; Sodium: 648mg; Total Carbohydrates: 29g; Dietary Fiber: 1g; Total Sugars: 10g; Protein: 12g

Cholula Avocado Fries

Servings: 2 | Prep Time: 10 Minutes | Cooking Time: 20 Minutes

Ingredients:

- 1 egg, beaten
- ¼ cup flour
- 2 tbsp ground flaxseed
- ¼ tsp Cholula sauce
- Salt to taste
- 1 avocado, cut into fries

Directions:

1. Preheat air fryer to 190°C/375°F. Mix the egg and Cholula sauce in a bowl. In another bowl, combine the remaining ingredients, except for the avocado. Submerge avocado slices in the egg mixture and dredge them into the flour to coat. Place the fries in the lightly greased frying basket and Air Fry for 5 minutes. Serve immediately.

Variations & Ingredients Tips:

- Use panko breadcrumbs instead of flaxseed for a crunchier coating.

- Dip the fries in ranch dressing or chipotle mayo.
- Sprinkle with chili-lime seasoning or everything bagel spice after cooking.

Per Serving: Calories: 243; Total Fat: 17g; Saturated Fat: 3g; Cholesterol: 93mg; Sodium: 154mg; Total Carbs: 19g; Dietary Fiber: 8g; Total Sugars: 1g; Protein: 7g

Cheese Straws

Servings: 8 | Prep Time: 15 Minutes | Cooking Time: 7 Minutes

Ingredients:

- For dusting All-purpose flour
- Two quarters of one thawed sheet (that is, a half of the sheet cut into two even pieces; wrap and refreeze the remainder) A 490 g box frozen puff pastry
- 1 Large egg(s)
- 2 tablespoons Water
- ¼ cup (about 20 g) Finely grated Parmesan cheese
- up to 1 teaspoon Ground black pepper

Directions:

1. Preheat the air fryer to 200°C/400°F.
2. Dust a clean, dry work surface with flour. Set one of the pieces of puff pastry on top, dust the pastry lightly with flour, and roll with a rolling pin to a 15 cm square.
3. Whisk the egg(s) and water in a small or medium bowl until uniform. Brush the pastry square(s) generously with this mixture. Sprinkle each square with 2 tablespoons grated cheese and up to ½ teaspoon ground black pepper.
4. Cut each square into 4 even strips. Grasp each end of 1 strip with clean, dry hands; twist it into a cheese straw. Place the twisted straws on a baking sheet.
5. Lay as many straws as will fit in the air-fryer basket—as a general rule, 4 of them in a small machine, 5 in a medium model, or 6 in a large. There should be space for air to circulate around the straws. Set the baking sheet with any remaining straws in the fridge.
6. Air-fry undisturbed for 7 minutes, or until puffed and crisp. Use tongs to transfer the cheese straws to a wire rack, then make subsequent batches in the same way (keeping the baking sheet with the remaining straws in the fridge as each batch cooks). Serve warm.

Variations & Ingredients Tips:

- Add some smoked paprika, garlic powder or cayenne pepper to the cheese mixture.
- Brush with pesto or sun-dried tomato paste before sprinkling with cheese.
- Serve alongside soup, salad or as a party appetizer.

Per Serving: Calories: 157; Total Fat: 11g; Saturated Fat: 3g; Cholesterol: 27mg; Sodium: 117mg; Total Carbs: 11g; Dietary Fiber: 0g; Total Sugars: 0g; Protein: 4g

Mozzarella Sticks

Servings: 4 | Prep Time: 10 Minutes | Cooking Time: 5 Minutes

Ingredients:

- 1 egg
- 1 tbsp water
- 8 eggroll wraps
- 8 mozzarella string cheese "sticks"
- sauce for dipping

Directions:

1. Beat together egg and water in a small bowl. Lay out egg roll wraps and moisten edges with egg wash. Place one piece of string cheese on each wrap near one end. Fold in sides of egg roll wrap over ends of cheese, and then roll up. Brush outside of wrap with egg wash and press gently to seal well. Place in air fryer basket in single layer and cook at 200°C/390°F for 5 minutes. Cook an additional 1 or 2 minutes, if necessary, until they are golden brown and crispy. Serve with your favorite dipping sauce.

Variations & Ingredients Tips:

- Use wonton wrappers instead of egg roll wraps for a lighter, crispier texture.
- Experiment with different types of cheese like cheddar, pepper jack, or gouda.
- Serve with ranch dressing, marinara sauce, or garlic aioli for dipping.

Per Serving: Calories: 218; Total Fat: 9g; Saturated Fat: 4g; Cholesterol: 71mg; Sodium: 552mg; Total Carbs: 23g; Dietary Fiber: 1g; Total Sugars: 1g; Protein: 12g

Kale Chips

Servings: 2 | Prep Time: 5 Minutes | Cooking Time: 5 Minutes

Ingredients:

- 4 Medium kale leaves, about 30 g each
- 2 teaspoons Olive oil
- 2 teaspoons Regular or low-sodium soy sauce or gluten-free tamari sauce

Directions:

1. Preheat the air fryer to 200°C/400°F.
2. Cut the stems from the leaves (all the stems, all the way up the leaf). Tear each leaf into three pieces. Put them in a large bowl.
3. Add the olive oil and soy or tamari sauce. Toss well to coat. You can even gently rub the leaves along the side of the bowl to get the liquids to stick to them.
4. When the machine is at temperature, put the leaf pieces in the basket in one layer. Air-fry for 5 minutes, turning and rearranging with kitchen tongs once halfway through, until the chips are dried out and crunchy. Watch carefully so

they don't turn dark brown at the edges.
5. Gently pour the contents of the basket onto a wire rack. Cool for at least 5 minutes before serving. The chips can keep for up to 8 hours uncovered on the rack (provided it's not a humid day).

Variations & Ingredients Tips:

- Use collard greens, Swiss chard or spinach instead of kale.
- Season with garlic powder, smoked paprika or nutritional yeast.
- Store leftovers in an airtight container at room temperature for up to 3 days.

Per Serving: Calories: 75; Total Fat: 5g; Saturated Fat: 1g; Cholesterol: 0mg; Sodium: 237mg; Total Carbs: 6g; Dietary Fiber: 2g; Total Sugars: 1g; Protein: 3g

Poppy Seed Mini Hot Dog Rolls

Servings: 4 | Prep Time: 10 Minutes | Cooking Time: 25 Minutes

Ingredients:

- 8 small mini hot dogs
- 8 pastry dough sheets
- 1 tbsp vegetable oil
- 1 tbsp poppy seeds

Directions:

1. Preheat the air fryer to 175°C/350°F. Roll the mini hot dogs into a pastry dough sheet, wrapping them snugly. Brush the rolls with vegetable oil on all sides. Arrange them on the frying basket and sprinkle poppy seeds on top. Bake for 15 minutes until the pastry crust is golden brown. Serve.

Variations & Ingredients Tips:

- Use different types of sausages like bratwurst, Italian sausage, or chorizo for variety.
- Brush the rolls with beaten egg instead of oil for a shinier, golden finish.
- Serve with mustard, ketchup, or your favorite dipping sauce.

Per Serving: Calories: 298; Total Fat: 23g; Saturated Fat: 5g; Cholesterol: 15mg; Sodium: 417mg; Total Carbs: 17g; Dietary Fiber: 1g; Total Sugars: 1g; Protein: 6g

Crispy Tofu Bites

Servings: 4 | Prep Time: 15 Minutes | Cooking Time: 20 Minutes

Ingredients:

- 450 g Extra firm unflavored tofu
- Vegetable oil spray

Directions:

1. Wrap the piece of tofu in a triple layer of paper towels. Place it on a wooden cutting board and set a large pot on top of it to press out excess moisture. Set aside for 10 minutes.
2. Preheat the air fryer to 200°C/400°F.
3. Remove the pot and unwrap the tofu. Cut it into 2.5 cm cubes. Place these in a bowl and coat them generously with vegetable oil spray. Toss gently, then spray generously again before tossing, until all are glistening.
4. Gently pour the tofu pieces into the basket, spread them into as close to one layer as possible, and air-fry for 20 minutes, using kitchen tongs to gently rearrange the pieces at the 7- and 14-minute marks, until light brown and crisp.
5. Gently pour the tofu pieces onto a wire rack. Cool for 5 minutes before serving warm.

Variations & Ingredients Tips:

- Toss the cooked tofu bites with your favorite sauce like buffalo, teriyaki or sweet chili.
- Season the tofu with soy sauce, garlic powder, smoked paprika or nutritional yeast before cooking.
- Serve as an appetizer with dipping sauces or add to salads, stir-fries or grain bowls.

Per Serving: Calories: 128; Total Fat: 9g; Saturated Fat: 1g; Cholesterol: 0mg; Sodium: 9mg; Total Carbs: 2g; Dietary Fiber: 1g; Total Sugars: 0g; Protein: 10g

Poultry Recipes

Japanese-style Turkey Meatballs

Servings: 4 | Prep Time: 15 Minutes | Cooking Time: 25 Minutes

Ingredients:

- 600g ground turkey
- 1/4 cup panko bread crumbs
- 4 chopped scallions
- 1/4 cup chopped cilantro
- 1 egg

- 1 tbsp grated ginger
- 1 garlic clove, minced
- 3 tbsp shoyu
- 2 tsp toasted sesame oil
- 3/4 tsp salt
- 2 tbsp oyster sauce
- 2 tbsp fresh orange juice

Directions:

1. Add ground turkey, panko, 3 scallions, cilantro, egg, ginger, garlic, 1 tbsp of shoyu sauce, sesame oil, and salt in a bowl. Mix with hands until combined.
2. Divide the mixture into 12 equal parts and roll into balls.
3. Preheat air fryer to 190°C/380°F. Place the meatballs in the greased frying basket. Bake for about 9-11 minutes, flipping once until browned and cooked through. Repeat for all meatballs.
4. In a small saucepan over medium heat, add oyster sauce, orange juice and remaining shoyu sauce. Bring to a boil, then reduce the heat to low. Cook until the sauce is slightly reduced, 3 minutes.
5. Serve the meatballs with the oyster sauce drizzled over them and topped with the remaining scallions.

Variations & Ingredients Tips:

- Use ground chicken or pork instead of turkey.
- Add some Sriracha to the sauce for heat.
- Serve as an appetizer with toothpicks or in a bahn mi sandwich.

Per Serving: Calories: 330; Total Fat: 17g; Saturated Fat: 4g; Cholesterol: 130mg; Sodium: 1350mg; Total Carbs: 9g; Dietary Fiber: 1g; Total Sugars: 4g; Protein: 35g

Crispy Cordon Bleu

Servings: 4 | Prep Time: 20 Minutes | Cooking Time: 25 Minutes

Ingredients:

- 4 deli ham slices, halved lengthwise
- 2 tbsp grated Parmesan
- 4 chicken breast halves
- Salt and pepper to taste
- 8 Swiss cheese slices
- 1 egg
- 2 egg whites
- ¾ cup bread crumbs
- 1 tsp garlic powder
- 1 tsp onion powder
- 1 tsp mustard powder

Directions:

1. Preheat air fryer to 200°C/400°F.
2. Season the chicken cutlets with salt and pepper. On one cutlet, put a half slice of ham and cheese on the top. Roll the chicken tightly, then set aside.
3. Beat the eggs and egg whites in a shallow bowl. Put the crumbs, Parmesan, garlic, onion, and mustard powder, in a second bowl.
4. Dip the cutlet in the egg bowl and then in the crumb mix. Press so that they stick to the chicken.
5. Put the rolls of chicken seam side down in the greased air fryer basket and Air Fry for 12-14 minutes, flipping once until golden and cooked through.
6. Serve.

Variations & Ingredients Tips:

- Use prosciutto, turkey, or bacon instead of ham for different flavors.
- Add a dollop of Dijon mustard or pesto inside each roll for extra flavor.
- Serve with a side of steamed vegetables or roasted potatoes.

Per Serving: Calories: 450; Total Fat: 20g; Saturated Fat: 9g; Sodium: 880mg; Total Carbohydrates: 18g; Dietary Fiber: 1g; Total Sugars: 2g; Protein: 48g

Indian Chicken Tandoori

Servings: 2 | Prep Time: 10 Minutes (plus Marinating Time) | Cooking Time: 35 Minutes

Ingredients:

- 2 chicken breasts, cubed
- 1/2 cup hung curd
- 1 tsp turmeric powder
- 1 tsp red chili powder
- 1 tsp chaat masala powder
- Pinch of salt

Directions:

1. Preheat air fryer to 175°C/350°F.
2. Mix the hung curd, turmeric, red chili powder, chaat masala powder, and salt in a mixing bowl. Stir until the mixture is free of lumps.
3. Coat the chicken with the mixture, cover, and refrigerate for 30 minutes to marinate.
4. Place the marinated chicken chunks in a baking pan and drizzle with the remaining marinade.
5. Bake for 25 minutes until the chicken is juicy and spiced.
6. Serve warm.

Variations & Ingredients Tips:

- Use Greek yogurt instead of hung curd for a tangy flavor.
- Add minced garlic and ginger to the marinade for extra zing.
- Garnish with fresh cilantro and squeeze of lime juice.

Per Serving: Calories: 220; Total Fat: 3g; Saturated Fat: 1g; Cholesterol: 105mg; Sodium: 370mg; Total Carbs: 4g; Dietary Fiber: 1g; Total Sugars: 2g; Protein: 41g

Gruyère Asparagus & Chicken Quiche

Servings: 4 | Prep Time: 15 Minutes | Cooking Time: 30 Minutes

Ingredients:

- 1 grilled chicken breast, diced
- 1/2 cup (55g) shredded Gruyère cheese
- 1 premade pie crust
- 2 eggs, beaten
- 1/4 cup milk
- Salt and pepper to taste
- 225g asparagus, sliced
- 1 lemon, zested

Directions:
1. Preheat air fryer to 180°C/360°F.
2. Carefully press the crust into a baking dish, trimming the edges. Prick the dough with a fork a few times.
3. Add the eggs, milk, asparagus, salt, pepper, chicken, lemon zest, and half of Gruyère cheese to a mixing bowl and stir until completely blended. Pour the mixture into the pie crust.
4. Bake in the air fryer for 15 minutes. Sprinkle the remaining Gruyère cheese on top of the quiche filling. Bake for 5 more minutes until the quiche is golden brown.
5. Remove and allow to cool for a few minutes before cutting. Serve sliced and enjoy!

Variations & Ingredients Tips:
- Use Swiss or cheddar cheese instead of Gruyère.
- Add sautéed mushrooms or spinach to the filling.
- Make a crustless quiche for a low-carb option.

Per Serving: Calories: 330; Total Fat: 22g; Saturated Fat: 10g; Cholesterol: 150mg; Sodium: 420mg; Total Carbs: 16g; Dietary Fiber: 1g; Total Sugars: 2g; Protein: 18g

Asian Meatball Tacos

Servings: 4 | Prep Time: 15 Minutes | Cooking Time: 10 Minutes

Ingredients:
- 450g lean ground turkey
- 3 tablespoons soy sauce
- 1 tablespoon brown sugar
- 1/2 teaspoon onion powder
- 1/2 teaspoon garlic powder
- 1 tablespoon sesame seeds
- 1 English cucumber
- 4 radishes
- 2 tablespoons white wine vinegar
- 1 lime, juiced and divided
- 1 tablespoon avocado oil
- Salt, to taste
- 1/2 cup Greek yogurt
- 1 to 3 teaspoons Sriracha, based on desired spiciness
- 1 cup shredded cabbage
- 1/4 cup chopped cilantro
- Eight 15-cm flour tortillas

Directions:
1. Preheat the air fryer to 180°C/360°F.
2. In a large bowl, mix the ground turkey, soy sauce, brown sugar, onion powder, garlic powder, and sesame seeds. Form the meat into 5cm meatballs and place in the air fryer basket.
3. Cook for 5 minutes, shake the basket, and cook another 5 minutes. Using a food thermometer, make sure the internal temperature of the meatballs is 75°C/165°F.
4. Meanwhile, dice the cucumber and radishes and place in a medium bowl. Add the white wine vinegar, 1 teaspoon of the lime juice, and the avocado oil, and stir to coat. Season with salt to desired taste.
5. In a large bowl, mix the Greek yogurt, Sriracha, and the remaining lime juice, and stir. Add in the cabbage and cilantro; toss well to create a slaw.
6. In a heavy skillet, heat the tortillas over medium heat for 1 to 2 minutes on each side, or until warmed.
7. To serve, place a tortilla on a plate, top with 5 meatballs, then with cucumber and radish salad, and finish with 2 tablespoons of cabbage slaw.

Variations & Ingredients Tips:
- Use ground chicken or pork instead of turkey for the meatballs.
- Swap flour tortillas for corn or lettuce wraps.
- Add shredded carrots to the slaw for extra crunch.

Per Serving: Calories: 440; Total Fat: 16g; Saturated Fat: 4g; Cholesterol: 110mg; Sodium: 900mg; Total Carbs: 46g; Dietary Fiber: 4g; Total Sugars: 10g; Protein: 29g

Mexican-inspired Chicken Breasts

Servings: 4 | Prep Time: 10 Minutes | Cooking Time: 20 Minutes

Ingredients:
- 1/8 tsp crushed red pepper flakes
- 1 red pepper, deseeded and diced
- Salt to taste
- 4 chicken breasts
- 3/4 tsp garlic powder
- 1/2 tsp onion powder
- 1/2 tsp ground cumin
- 1/2 tsp ancho chile powder
- 1/2 tsp sweet paprika
- 1/2 tsp Mexican oregano
- 1 tomato, chopped
- 1/2 diced red onion
- 3 tbsp fresh lime juice
- 285g avocado, diced
- 1 tbsp chopped cilantro

Directions:
1. Preheat air fryer to 190°C/380°F.
2. Stir together salt, garlic and onion powder, cumin, ancho chili powder, paprika, Mexican oregano, and pepper flakes in a bowl.
3. Spray the chicken with cooking oil and rub with the spice mix. Air Fry the chicken for 10 minutes, flipping once until browned and fully cooked. Repeat for all of the chicken.
4. Mix the onion and lime juice in a bowl. Fold in the avocado, cilantro, red pepper, salt, and tomato and coat gently.
5. To serve, top the chicken with guacamole salsa.

Variations & Ingredients Tips:
- Use boneless, skinless chicken thighs for juicier meat.
- Add some crumbled cotija or feta cheese on top.

- Serve sliced over a bed of rice and black beans.

Per Serving: Calories: 400; Total Fat: 22g; Saturated Fat: 4g; Cholesterol: 145mg; Sodium: 420mg; Total Carbs: 10g; Dietary Fiber: 6g; Total Sugars: 3g; Protein: 44g

Fiesta Chicken Plate

Servings: 4 | Prep Time: 10 Minutes | Cooking Time: 15 Minutes

Ingredients:

- 450g boneless, skinless chicken breasts (2 large breasts)
- 2 tablespoons lime juice
- 1 teaspoon cumin
- 1/2 teaspoon salt
- 1/2 cup grated Pepper Jack cheese
- 1 (450g) can refried beans
- 1/2 cup salsa
- 2 cups shredded lettuce
- 1 medium tomato, chopped
- 2 avocados, peeled and sliced
- 1 small onion, sliced into thin rings
- Sour cream
- Tortilla chips (optional)

Directions:

1. Split each chicken breast in half lengthwise.
2. Mix lime juice, cumin, and salt together and brush on all surfaces of chicken breasts.
3. Place in air fryer basket and cook at 200°C/390°F for 15 minutes, until well done.
4. Divide the cheese evenly over chicken breasts and cook for an additional minute to melt cheese.
5. While chicken is cooking, heat refried beans on stovetop or in microwave.
6. When ready to serve, divide beans among 4 plates. Place chicken breasts on top of beans and spoon salsa over. Arrange the lettuce, tomatoes, and avocados artfully on each plate and scatter with the onion rings.
7. Pass sour cream at the table and serve with tortilla chips if desired.

Variations & Ingredients Tips:

- Substitute Pepper Jack with Monterey Jack or cheddar cheese.
- Add some pickled jalapeños or hot sauce for extra spice.
- Use black beans instead of refried for more texture.

Per Serving: Calories: 550; Total Fat: 32g; Saturated Fat: 8g; Cholesterol: 105mg; Sodium: 920mg; Total Carbs: 35g; Dietary Fiber: 12g; Total Sugars: 4g; Protein: 38g

Kale & Rice Chicken Rolls

Servings: 4 | Prep Time: 15 Minutes | Cooking Time: 35 Minutes

Ingredients:

- 4 boneless, skinless chicken thighs
- 1/2 tsp ground fenugreek seeds
- 1 cup cooked wild rice
- 2 sundried tomatoes, diced
- 1/2 cup chopped kale
- 2 garlic cloves, minced
- 1 tsp salt
- 1 lemon, juiced
- 1/2 cup crumbled feta
- 1 tbsp olive oil

Directions:

1. Preheat air fryer to 190°C/380°F.
2. Put the chicken thighs between two pieces of plastic wrap, and using a meat mallet or a rolling pin, pound them out to about 6-mm thick.
3. Combine the rice, tomatoes, kale, garlic, salt, fenugreek seeds and lemon juice in a bowl and mix well.
4. Divide the rice mixture among the chicken thighs and sprinkle with feta. Fold the sides of the chicken thigh over the filling, and then gently place each of them seam-side down into the greased air frying basket. Drizzle the stuffed chicken thighs with olive oil.
5. Roast the stuffed chicken thighs for 12 minutes, then turn them over and cook for an additional 10 minutes.
6. Serve and enjoy!

Variations & Ingredients Tips:

- Use spinach or chard instead of kale.
- Add some chopped nuts like pistachios or pine nuts to the filling.
- Drizzle with tzatziki sauce before serving.

Per Serving: Calories: 370; Total Fat: 21g; Saturated Fat: 7g; Cholesterol: 145mg; Sodium: 900mg; Total Carbs: 17g; Dietary Fiber: 2g; Total Sugars: 2g; Protein: 32g

Chicken Meatballs With A Surprise

Servings: 4 | Prep Time: 15 Minutes | Cooking Time: 35 Minutes

Ingredients:

- 1/3 cup cottage cheese crumbles
- 450g ground chicken
- 1/2 tsp onion powder
- 1/4 cup chopped basil
- 1/2 cup bread crumbs
- 1/2 tsp garlic powder

Directions:

1. Preheat air fryer to 175°C/350°F.
2. Combine the ground chicken, onion powder, basil, cottage cheese, bread crumbs, and garlic powder in a bowl.
3. Form into 18 meatballs, about 2 tbsp each.
4. Place the chicken meatballs in the greased frying basket and Air Fry for 12 minutes, shaking once.
5. Serve.

Variations & Ingredients Tips:

- Use ground turkey instead of chicken.
- Add grated parmesan or shredded mozzarella cheese.
- Serve meatballs with marinara sauce for dipping.

Per Serving (4-5 meatballs): Calories: 230; Total Fat: 8g; Saturated Fat: 2g; Cholesterol: 106mg; Sodium: 384mg; Total Carbs: 14g; Dietary Fiber: 1g; Total Sugars: 1g; Protein: 25g

Cajun Fried Chicken

Servings: 3 | Prep Time: 10 Minutes | Cooking Time: 35 Minutes

Ingredients:

- 1 cup Cajun seasoning
- ½ tsp mango powder
- 6 chicken legs, bone-in

Directions:

1. Preheat air fryer to 180°C/360°F.
2. Place half of the Cajun seasoning and 3/4 cup of water in a bowl and mix well to dissolve any lumps.
3. Add the remaining Cajun seasoning and mango powder to a shallow bowl and stir to combine.
4. Dip the chicken in the batter, then coat it in the mango seasoning. Lightly spritz the chicken with cooking spray.
5. Place the chicken in the air fryer and Air Fry for 14-16 minutes, turning once until the chicken is cooked and the coating is brown.
6. Serve and enjoy!

Variations & Ingredients Tips:

- Use chicken wings, thighs, or breasts instead of legs.
- Adjust the amount of Cajun seasoning to make it spicier or milder.
- Serve with a side of coleslaw, potato salad, or corn on the cob.

Per Serving: Calories: 460; Total Fat: 26g; Saturated Fat: 7g; Sodium: 2270mg; Total Carbohydrates: 9g; Dietary Fiber: 3g; Total Sugars: 1g; Protein: 45g

Creole Chicken Drumettes

Servings: 4 | Prep Time: 20 Minutes | Cooking Time: 50 Minutes

Ingredients:

- 454 grams chicken drumettes
- ½ cup flour
- ½ cup heavy cream
- ½ cup sour cream
- ½ cup bread crumbs
- 1 tbsp Creole seasoning
- 2 tbsp melted butter

Directions:

1. Preheat air fryer to 190°C/370°F.
2. Combine chicken drumettes and flour in a bowl. Shake away excess flour and set aside.
3. Mix the heavy cream and sour cream in a bowl.
4. In another bowl, combine bread crumbs and Creole seasoning.
5. Dip floured drumettes in cream mixture, then dredge them in crumbs.
6. Place the chicken drumettes in the greased air fryer basket and Air Fry for 20 minutes, tossing once and brushing with melted butter.
7. Let rest for a few minutes on a plate and serve.

Variations & Ingredients Tips:

- Use chicken wings or drumsticks instead of drumettes.
- Add cayenne pepper, paprika, or garlic powder to the bread crumb mixture for extra spice.
- Serve with ranch dressing, blue cheese dip, or hot sauce on the side.

Per Serving: Calories: 480; Total Fat: 34g; Saturated Fat: 18g; Sodium: 610mg; Total Carbohydrates: 21g; Dietary Fiber: 1g; Total Sugars: 2g; Protein: 25g

Buffalo Egg Rolls

Servings: 8 | Prep Time: 20 Minutes | Cooking Time: 9 Minutes Per Batch

Ingredients:

- 1 teaspoon water
- 1 tablespoon cornstarch
- 1 egg
- 2½ cups cooked chicken, diced or shredded (see opposite page)
- ⅓ cup chopped green onion
- ⅓ cup diced celery
- ⅓ cup buffalo wing sauce
- 8 egg roll wraps
- oil for misting or cooking spray
- Blue Cheese Dip
- 85 grams cream cheese, softened
- ⅓ cup blue cheese, crumbled
- 1 teaspoon Worcestershire sauce
- ¼ teaspoon garlic powder
- ¼ cup buttermilk (or sour cream)

Directions:

1. Mix water and cornstarch in a small bowl until dissolved. Add egg, beat well, and set aside.
2. In a medium size bowl, mix together chicken, green onion, celery, and buffalo wing sauce.
3. Divide chicken mixture evenly among 8 egg roll wraps, spooning 1 cm from one edge.
4. Moisten all edges of each wrap with beaten egg wash.
5. Fold the short ends over filling, then roll up tightly and press to seal edges.
6. Brush outside of wraps with egg wash, then spritz with oil or cooking spray.
7. Place 4 egg rolls in air fryer basket.

28

8. Cook at 200°C/390°F for 9 minutes or until outside is brown and crispy.
9. While the rolls are cooking, prepare the Blue Cheese Dip. With a fork, mash together cream cheese and blue cheese.
10. Stir in remaining ingredients.
11. Dip should be just thick enough to slightly cling to egg rolls. If too thick, stir in buttermilk or milk 1 tablespoon at a time until you reach the desired consistency.
12. Cook remaining 4 egg rolls as in steps 7 and 8.
13. Serve while hot with Blue Cheese Dip, more buffalo wing sauce, or both.

Variations & Ingredients Tips:

- Use boneless, skinless chicken breasts or turkey instead of pre-cooked chicken.
- Substitute buffalo sauce with BBQ sauce, teriyaki sauce, or sweet chili sauce.
- Serve with ranch or bleu cheese dressing for dipping.

Per Serving: Calories: 280; Total Fat: 16g; Saturated Fat: 6g; Sodium: 620mg; Total Carbohydrates: 18g; Dietary Fiber: 1g; Total Sugars: 1g; Protein: 16g

Teriyaki Chicken Legs

Servings: 2 | Prep Time: 5 Minutes | Cooking Time: 20 Minutes

Ingredients:

- 4 tablespoons teriyaki sauce
- 1 tablespoon orange juice
- 1 teaspoon smoked paprika
- 4 chicken legs
- Cooking spray

Directions:

1. Mix together teriyaki sauce, orange juice and smoked paprika.
2. Brush sauce mixture on all sides of chicken legs.
3. Spray air fryer basket with cooking spray and add chicken legs.
4. Cook at 180°C/360°F for 6 mins. Turn and baste with sauce.
5. Cook 6 more mins, turn and baste again.
6. Cook 8 additional mins until juices run clear when pierced.

Variations & Ingredients Tips:

- Use chicken thighs or drumsticks instead of whole legs.
- Add garlic powder, ginger or honey to the teriyaki sauce.
- Brush with extra sauce after cooking and broil 2-3 mins for caramelization.

Per Serving (2 legs): Calories: 383; Total Fat: 18g; Saturated Fat: 4g; Cholesterol: 194mg; Sodium: 1096mg; Total Carbs: 15g; Dietary Fiber: 0g; Total Sugars: 10g; Protein: 41g

Curried Chicken Legs

Servings: 4 | Prep Time: 10 Minutes (plus Marinating Time) | Cooking Time: 40 Minutes

Ingredients:

- ¾ cup Greek yogurt
- 1 tbsp tomato paste
- 2 tsp curry powder
- ½ tbsp oregano
- 1 tsp salt
- 680 grams chicken legs
- 2 tbsp chopped fresh mint

Directions:

1. Combine yogurt, tomato paste, curry powder, oregano and salt in a bowl. Divide the mixture in half. Cover one half and store it in the fridge. Into the other half, toss in the chicken until coated and marinate covered in the fridge for 30 minutes up to overnight.
2. Preheat air fryer to 190°C/370°F.
3. Shake excess marinade from chicken. Place chicken legs in the greased air fryer basket and Air Fry for 18 minutes, flipping once and brushing with yogurt mixture.
4. Serve topped with mint.

Variations & Ingredients Tips:

- Use chicken drumsticks or thighs instead of legs.
- Add minced garlic, ginger, or cayenne pepper to the marinade for extra spice.
- Serve with basmati rice, naan bread, and cucumber raita on the side.

Per Serving: Calories: 350; Total Fat: 20g; Saturated Fat: 6g; Sodium: 620mg; Total Carbohydrates: 4g; Dietary Fiber: 1g; Total Sugars: 2g; Protein: 36g

Chicken Schnitzel Dogs

Servings: 4 | Prep Time: 20 Minutes | Cooking Time: 10 Minutes

Ingredients:

- ½ cup flour
- ½ teaspoon salt
- 1 teaspoon marjoram
- 1 teaspoon dried parsley flakes
- ½ teaspoon thyme
- 1 egg
- 1 teaspoon lemon juice
- 1 teaspoon water
- 1 cup breadcrumbs
- 4 chicken tenders, pounded thin
- oil for misting or cooking spray
- 4 whole-grain hotdog buns
- 4 slices Gouda cheese
- 1 small Granny Smith apple, thinly sliced
- ½ cup shredded Napa cabbage
- coleslaw dressing

Directions:

1. In a shallow dish, mix together the flour, salt, marjoram,

parsley, and thyme.
2. In another shallow dish, beat together egg, lemon juice, and water.
3. Place breadcrumbs in a third shallow dish.
4. Cut each of the flattened chicken tenders in half lengthwise.
5. Dip flattened chicken strips in flour mixture, then egg wash. Let excess egg drip off and roll in breadcrumbs. Spray both sides with oil or cooking spray.
6. Cook at 200°C/390°F for 5 minutes. Spray with oil, turn over, and spray other side.
7. Cook for 3 to 5 minutes more, until well done and crispy brown.
8. To serve, place 2 schnitzel strips on bottom of each hot dog bun. Top with cheese, sliced apple, and cabbage. Drizzle with coleslaw dressing and top with other half of bun.

Variations & Ingredients Tips:

- Use turkey or pork cutlets instead of chicken for different schnitzel options.
- Add sauerkraut, pickles, or mustard for German-style toppings.
- Serve with a side of potato salad or French fries.

Per Serving: Calories: 480; Total Fat: 20g; Saturated Fat: 6g; Sodium: 1020mg; Total Carbohydrates: 48g; Dietary Fiber: 6g; Total Sugars: 9g; Protein: 31g

Chicken Breast Burgers

Servings: 4 | Prep Time: 10 Minutes (plus 30 Minutes Marinating Time) | Cooking Time: 35 Minutes

Ingredients:

- 2 chicken breasts
- 1 cup dill pickle juice
- 1 cup buttermilk
- 1 egg
- ½ cup flour
- Salt and pepper to taste
- 4 buns
- 2 pickles, sliced

Directions:

1. Cut the chicken into cutlets by cutting them in half horizontally on a cutting board. Transfer them to a large bowl along with pickle juice and ½ cup of buttermilk. Toss to coat, then marinate for 30 minutes in the fridge.
2. Preheat air fryer to 190°C/370°F.
3. In a shallow bowl, beat the egg and the rest of the buttermilk to combine. In another shallow bowl, mix flour, salt, and pepper.
4. Dip the marinated cutlet in the egg mixture, then dredge in flour.
5. Place the cutlets in the greased air fryer basket and Air Fry for 12 minutes, flipping once halfway through.
6. Remove the cutlets and pickles on buns and serve.

Variations & Ingredients Tips:

- Use boneless, skinless chicken thighs instead of breasts for juicier meat.
- Add garlic powder, onion powder, or paprika to the flour mixture for extra seasoning.
- Top with sliced tomato, lettuce, avocado, or cheese for a loaded burger.

Per Serving: Calories: 420; Total Fat: 13g; Saturated Fat: 3.5g; Sodium: 1090mg; Total Carbohydrates: 43g; Dietary Fiber: 2g; Total Sugars: 8g; Protein: 34g

Crispy Chicken Parmesan

Servings: 4 | Prep Time: 15 Minutes | Cooking Time: 12 Minutes

Ingredients:

- 4 skinless, boneless chicken breasts, pounded thin to 0.6-cm thickness
- 1 teaspoon salt, divided
- ½ teaspoon black pepper, divided
- 1 cup flour
- 2 eggs
- 1 cup panko breadcrumbs
- ½ teaspoon dried oregano
- ½ cup grated Parmesan cheese

Directions:

1. Pat the chicken breasts with a paper towel. Season the chicken with ½ teaspoon of the salt and ¼ teaspoon of the pepper.
2. In a medium bowl, place the flour.
3. In a second bowl, whisk the eggs.
4. In a third bowl, place the breadcrumbs, oregano, cheese, and the remaining ½ teaspoon of salt and ¼ teaspoon of pepper.
5. Dredge the chicken in the flour and shake off the excess. Dip the chicken into the eggs and then into the breadcrumbs. Set the chicken on a plate and repeat with the remaining chicken pieces.
6. Preheat the air fryer to 180°C/360°F.
7. Place the chicken in the air fryer basket and spray liberally with cooking spray. Cook for 8 minutes, turn the chicken breasts over, and cook another 4 minutes. When golden brown, check for an internal temperature of 75°C/165°F.

Variations & Ingredients Tips:

- Use chicken thighs or cutlets instead of breasts for juicier meat.
- Add garlic powder, onion powder, or Italian seasoning to the breadcrumb mixture for extra flavor.
- Serve with marinara sauce, pesto, or a side of spaghetti for a complete meal.

Per Serving: Calories: 410; Total Fat: 11g; Saturated Fat: 4g; Sodium: 880mg; Total Carbohydrates: 35g; Dietary Fiber: 2g; Total Sugars: 2g; Protein: 44g

Bacon & Chicken Flatbread

Servings: 2 | Prep Time: 20 Minutes | Cooking Time: 35 Minutes

Ingredients:

- 1 flatbread dough
- 1 chicken breast, cubed
- 1 cup breadcrumbs
- 2 eggs, beaten
- Salt and pepper to taste
- 2 tsp dry rosemary
- 1 tsp fajita seasoning
- 1 tsp onion powder
- 3 bacon strips
- ½ tbsp ranch sauce

Directions:

1. Preheat air fryer to 180°C/360°F.
2. Place the breadcrumbs, onion powder, rosemary, salt, and pepper in a mixing bowl. Coat the chicken with the mixture, dip into the beaten eggs, then roll again into the dry ingredients.
3. Arrange the coated chicken pieces on one side of the greased air fryer basket. On the other side of the basket, lay the bacon strips.
4. Air Fry for 6 minutes. Turn the bacon pieces over and flip the chicken and cook for another 6 minutes.
5. Roll the flatbread out and spread the ranch sauce all over the surface. Top with the bacon and chicken and sprinkle with fajita seasoning.
6. Close the bread to contain the filling and place it in the air fryer. Cook for 10 minutes, flipping the flatbread once until golden brown.
7. Let it cool for a few minutes. Then slice and serve.

Variations & Ingredients Tips:

- Use turkey bacon or prosciutto instead of regular bacon for a leaner option.
- Add sliced avocado, tomatoes, or lettuce to the flatbread for extra veggies.
- Substitute ranch sauce with BBQ sauce, honey mustard, or hot sauce for different flavors.

Per Serving: Calories: 580; Total Fat: 23g; Saturated Fat: 6g; Sodium: 1180mg; Total Carbohydrates: 58g; Dietary Fiber: 3g; Total Sugars: 4g; Protein: 38g

Sweet Nutty Chicken Breasts

Servings: 4 | Prep Time: 10 Minutes | Cooking Time: 30 Minutes

Ingredients:

- 2 chicken breasts, halved lengthwise
- 1/4 cup honey mustard
- 1/4 cup chopped pecans
- 1 tbsp olive oil
- 1 tbsp parsley, chopped

Directions:

1. Preheat air fryer to 175°C/350°F.
2. Brush chicken breasts with honey mustard and olive oil on all sides.
3. Place the pecans in a bowl. Add and coat the chicken breasts.
4. Place the breasts in the greased frying basket and Air Fry for 25 minutes, turning once.
5. Let chill onto a serving plate for 5 minutes. Sprinkle with parsley and serve.

Variations & Ingredients Tips:

- Use other nuts like almonds or walnuts instead of pecans.
- Add dried herbs like thyme or rosemary to the nut coating.
- Serve with a honey mustard dipping sauce on the side.

Per Serving: Calories: 307; Total Fat: 14g; Saturated Fat: 2g; Cholesterol: 88mg; Sodium: 237mg; Total Carbs: 14g; Dietary Fiber: 1g; Total Sugars: 10g; Protein: 31g

Chicken Rochambeau

Servings: 4 | Prep Time: 15 Minutes | Cooking Time: 20 Minutes

Ingredients:

- 1 tablespoon butter
- 4 chicken tenders, cut in half crosswise
- salt and pepper
- ¼ cup flour
- oil for misting
- 4 slices ham, 0.6- to 1-cm thick and large enough to cover an English muffin
- 2 English muffins, split
- Sauce
- 2 tablespoons butter
- ½ cup chopped green onions
- ½ cup chopped mushrooms
- 2 tablespoons flour
- 1 cup chicken broth
- ¼ teaspoon garlic powder
- 1½ teaspoons Worcestershire sauce

Directions:

1. Place 1 tablespoon of butter in air fryer baking pan and cook at 200°C/390°F for 2 minutes to melt.
2. Sprinkle chicken tenders with salt and pepper to taste, then roll in the ¼ cup of flour.
3. Place chicken in baking pan, turning pieces to coat with melted butter.
4. Cook at 200°C/390°F for 5 minutes. Turn chicken pieces over, and spray tops lightly with olive oil. Cook 5 minutes longer or until juices run clear. The chicken will not brown.
5. While chicken is cooking, make the sauce: In a medium saucepan, melt the 2 tablespoons of butter.
6. Add onions and mushrooms and sauté until tender, about 3 minutes.
7. Stir in the flour. Gradually add broth, stirring constantly until you have a smooth gravy.
8. Add garlic powder and Worcestershire sauce and simmer on low heat until sauce thickens, about 5 minutes.

9. When chicken is cooked, remove baking pan from air fryer and set aside.
10. Place ham slices directly into air fryer basket and cook at 200°C/390°F for 5 minutes or until hot and beginning to sizzle a little. Remove and set aside on top of the chicken for now.
11. Place the English muffin halves in air fryer basket and cook at 200°C/390°F for 1 minute.
12. Open air fryer and place a ham slice on top of each English muffin half. Stack 2 pieces of chicken on top of each ham slice. Cook at 200°C/390°F for 1 to 2 minutes to heat through.
13. Place each English muffin stack on a serving plate and top with plenty of sauce.

Variations & Ingredients Tips:

- Use turkey or pork instead of chicken for different meats.
- Substitute English muffins with biscuits or toast.
- Add a slice of cheese on top of the ham for extra richness.

Per Serving: Calories: 430; Total Fat: 24g; Saturated Fat: 11g; Sodium: 1070mg; Total Carbohydrates: 27g; Dietary Fiber: 2g; Total Sugars: 3g; Protein: 29g

Basic Chicken Breasts

Servings: 4 | Prep Time: 5 Minutes | Cooking Time: 15 Minutes

Ingredients:

- 2 tsp olive oil
- 2 chicken breasts
- Salt and pepper to taste
- ½ tsp garlic powder
- ½ tsp rosemary

Directions:

1. Preheat air fryer to 180°C/350°F.
2. Rub the chicken breasts with olive oil over tops and bottom and sprinkle with garlic powder, rosemary, salt, and pepper.
3. Place the chicken in the air fryer basket and Air Fry for 9 minutes, flipping once.
4. Let rest onto a serving plate for 5 minutes before cutting into cubes.
5. Serve and enjoy!

Variations & Ingredients Tips:

- Use boneless, skinless chicken thighs instead of breasts for juicier meat.
- Add a pinch of paprika, oregano, or thyme for extra herb flavor.
- Slice the chicken and serve over salads, pasta, or sandwiches.

Per Serving: Calories: 150; Total Fat: 6g; Saturated Fat: 1g; Sodium: 75mg; Total Carbohydrates: 0g; Dietary Fiber: 0g; Total Sugars: 0g; Protein: 24g

Maewoon Chicken Legs

Servings: 4 | Prep Time: 10 Minutes | Cooking Time: 30 Minutes + Chilling Time

Ingredients:

- 4 scallions, sliced, whites and greens separated
- 1/4 cup tamari
- 2 tbsp sesame oil
- 1 tsp sesame seeds
- 1/4 cup honey
- 2 tbsp gochujang
- 2 tbsp ketchup
- 4 cloves garlic, minced
- 1/2 tsp ground ginger
- Salt and pepper to taste
- 1 tbsp parsley
- 680g chicken legs

Directions:

1. Whisk all ingredients, except chicken and scallion greens, in a bowl. Reserve 1/4 cup of marinade.
2. Toss chicken legs in the remaining marinade and chill for 30 minutes.
3. Preheat air fryer at 200°C/400°F. Place chicken legs in the greased frying basket and Air Fry for 10 minutes. Turn chicken. Cook for 8 more minutes.
4. Let sit in a serving dish for 5 minutes. Coat the cooked chicken with the reserved marinade and scatter with scallion greens, sesame seeds and parsley to serve.

Variations & Ingredients Tips:

- Use chicken wings or drumsticks instead of legs.
- Add a splash of rice vinegar or mirin to the marinade.
- Serve with steamed rice and kimchi.

Per Serving: Calories: 510; Total Fat: 32g; Saturated Fat: 8g; Cholesterol: 215mg; Sodium: 1510mg; Total Carbs: 23g; Dietary Fiber: 1g; Total Sugars: 19g; Protein: 35g

Jerk Turkey Meatballs

Servings: 7 | Prep Time: 15 Minutes | Cooking Time: 8 Minutes

Ingredients:

- 450g lean ground turkey
- 1/4 cup chopped onion
- 1 teaspoon minced garlic
- 1/2 teaspoon dried thyme
- 1/4 teaspoon ground cinnamon
- 1 teaspoon cayenne pepper
- 1/2 teaspoon paprika
- 1/2 teaspoon salt
- 1/8 teaspoon black pepper
- 1/4 teaspoon red pepper flakes
- 2 teaspoons brown sugar
- 1 large egg, whisked
- 1/3 cup panko breadcrumbs
- 2 1/3 cups cooked brown Jasmine rice
- 2 green onions, chopped
- 3/4 cup sweet onion dressing

Directions:

1. Preheat the air fryer to 175°C/350°F.
2. In a medium bowl, mix the ground turkey with the onion, garlic, thyme, cinnamon, cayenne pepper, paprika, salt, pepper, red pepper flakes, and brown sugar. Add the whisked egg and stir in the breadcrumbs until the turkey starts to hold together.
3. Using a 30-ml scoop, portion the turkey into meatballs. You should get about 28 meatballs.
4. Spray the air fryer basket with olive oil spray.
5. Place the meatballs into the air fryer basket and cook for 5 minutes, shake the basket, and cook another 2 to 4 minutes (or until the internal temperature of the meatballs reaches 74°C/165°F).
6. Remove the meatballs from the basket and repeat for the remaining meatballs.
7. Serve warm over a bed of rice with chopped green onions and spicy Caribbean jerk dressing.

Variations & Ingredients Tips:

- Use ground chicken or pork instead of turkey.
- Add diced bell peppers or carrots to the meatball mix.
- Serve in lettuce wraps or slider buns.

Per Serving: Calories: 300; Total Fat: 11g; Saturated Fat: 2.5g; Cholesterol: 85mg; Sodium: 450mg; Total Carbs: 28g; Dietary Fiber: 2g; Total Sugars: 5g; Protein: 22g

Parmesan Chicken Fingers

Servings: 2 | Prep Time: 15 Minutes | Cooking Time: 19 Minutes

Ingredients:

- 1/2 cup flour
- 1 teaspoon salt
- Freshly ground black pepper
- 2 eggs, beaten
- 3/4 cup seasoned panko breadcrumbs
- 3/4 cup grated Parmesan cheese
- 8 chicken tenders (about 450g) OR 2 to 3 boneless, skinless chicken breasts, cut into strips
- Vegetable oil
- Marinara sauce

Directions:

1. Set up a dredging station. Combine the flour, salt and pepper in a shallow dish. Place the beaten eggs in second shallow dish, and combine the panko breadcrumbs and Parmesan cheese in a third shallow dish.
2. Dredge the chicken tenders in the flour mixture. Then dip them into the egg, and finally place the chicken in the breadcrumb mixture. Press the coating onto both sides of the chicken tenders. Place the coated chicken tenders on a baking sheet until they are all coated. Spray both sides of the chicken fingers with vegetable oil.
3. Preheat the air fryer to 180°C/360°F.
4. Air-fry the chicken fingers in two batches. Transfer half the chicken fingers to the air fryer basket and air-fry for 9 minutes, turning the chicken over halfway through the cooking time. When the second batch of chicken fingers has finished cooking, return the first batch to the air fryer with the second batch and air-fry for one minute to heat everything through.
5. Serve immediately with marinara sauce, honey-mustard, ketchup or your favorite dipping sauce.

Variations & Ingredients Tips:

- Use almond flour and gluten-free breadcrumbs for a GF version.
- Add dried herbs or spices like oregano, paprika, or garlic powder to the breading.
- Serve over a salad or in a wrap with lettuce and tomato.

Per Serving: Calories: 600; Total Fat: 23g; Saturated Fat: 8g; Cholesterol: 270mg; Sodium: 1580mg; Total Carbs: 39g; Dietary Fiber: 2g; Total Sugars: 3g; Protein: 60g

Italian Roasted Chicken Thighs

Servings: 6 | Prep Time: 5 Minutes | Cooking Time: 14 Minutes

Ingredients:

- 6 boneless chicken thighs
- 1/2 teaspoon dried oregano
- 1/2 teaspoon garlic powder
- 1/2 teaspoon sea salt
- 1/2 teaspoon black pepper
- 1/4 teaspoon crushed red pepper flakes

Directions:

1. Pat the chicken thighs with paper towel.
2. In a small bowl, mix the oregano, garlic powder, salt, pepper, and crushed red pepper flakes. Rub the spice mixture onto the chicken thighs.
3. Preheat the air fryer to 200°C/400°F.
4. Place the chicken thighs in the air fryer basket and spray with cooking spray. Cook for 10 minutes, turn over, and cook another 4 minutes. When cooking completes, the internal temperature should read 75°C/165°F.

Variations & Ingredients Tips:

- Add some grated lemon zest to the spice mix for a bright flavor.
- Wrap each thigh with a slice of prosciutto before air frying.
- Serve over pasta, salad or roasted vegetables.

Per Serving: Calories: 210; Total Fat: 11g; Saturated Fat: 3g; Cholesterol: 140mg; Sodium: 390mg; Total Carbs: 0g; Dietary Fiber: 0g; Total Sugars: 0g; Protein: 28g

Sunday Chicken Skewers

Servings: 4 | Prep Time: 15 Minutes | Cooking Time: 25 Minutes

Ingredients:

- 1 green bell pepper, cut into chunks
- 1 red bell pepper, cut into chunks
- 4 chicken breasts, cubed
- 1 tbsp chicken seasoning
- Salt and pepper to taste
- 16 cherry tomatoes
- 8 pearl onions, peeled

Directions:

1. Preheat air fryer to 180°C/360°F.
2. Season the chicken cubes with chicken seasoning, salt, and pepper.
3. Thread metal skewers with chicken, bell pepper chunks, cherry tomatoes, and pearl onions.
4. Put the kabobs in the greased frying basket.
5. Bake for 14-16 minutes, flipping once until cooked through.
6. Let cool slightly. Serve.

Variations & Ingredients Tips:

- Use boneless, skinless chicken thighs for more flavor.
- Marinate the chicken in Italian dressing before threading.
- Add mushrooms, zucchini or pineapple chunks to the skewers.

Per Serving (2 skewers): Calories: 259; Total Fat: 4g; Saturated Fat: 1g; Cholesterol: 83mg; Sodium: 352mg; Total Carbs: 18g; Dietary Fiber: 3g; Total Sugars: 8g; Protein: 38g

Chicken & Rice Sautée

Servings: 4 | Prep Time: 15 Minutes | Cooking Time: 25 Minutes

Ingredients:

- 1 can pineapple chunks, drained, ¼ cup juice reserved
- 1 cup cooked long-grain rice
- 454 grams chicken breasts, cubed
- 1 red onion, chopped
- 1 tbsp peanut oil
- 1 peeled peach, cubed
- 1 tbsp cornstarch
- ½ tsp ground ginger
- ¼ tsp chicken seasoning

Directions:

1. Preheat air fryer to 200°C/400°F.
2. Combine the chicken, red onion, pineapple, and peanut oil in a metal bowl, then put the bowl in the fryer. Air Fry for 9 minutes, remove and stir.
3. Toss the peach in and put the bowl back into the fryer for 3 minutes. Slide out and stir again.
4. Mix the reserved pineapple juice, cornstarch, ginger, and chicken seasoning in a bowl, then pour over the chicken mixture and stir well.
5. Put the bowl back into the fryer and cook for 3 more minutes or until the chicken is cooked through and the sauce is thick.
6. Serve over cooked rice.

Variations & Ingredients Tips:

- Use shrimp, tofu, or pork instead of chicken for different protein options.
- Add sliced bell peppers, mushrooms, or snap peas for extra veggies.
- Serve with quinoa, couscous, or noodles instead of rice.

Per Serving: Calories: 350; Total Fat: 9g; Saturated Fat: 1.5g; Sodium: 150mg; Total Carbohydrates: 36g; Dietary Fiber: 3g; Total Sugars: 18g; Protein: 32g

Cornish Hens With Honey-lime Glaze

Servings: 2 | Prep Time: 10 Minutes | Cooking Time: 30 Minutes

Ingredients:

- 1 Cornish game hen (680-907 grams)
- 1 tablespoon honey
- 1 tablespoon lime juice
- 1 teaspoon poultry seasoning
- salt and pepper
- cooking spray

Directions:

1. To split the hen into halves, cut through breast bone and down one side of the backbone.
2. Mix the honey, lime juice, and poultry seasoning together and brush or rub onto all sides of the hen. Season to taste with salt and pepper.
3. Spray air fryer basket with cooking spray and place hen halves in the basket, skin-side down.
4. Cook at 165°C/330°F for 30 minutes. Hen will be done when juices run clear when pierced at leg joint with a fork.
5. Let hen rest for 5 to 10 minutes before cutting.

Variations & Ingredients Tips:

- Use orange juice, soy sauce, or balsamic vinegar instead of lime juice for different glazes.
- Add minced garlic, ginger, or red pepper flakes to the glaze for extra flavor.
- Stuff the hen cavity with lemon wedges, garlic cloves, or fresh herbs before cooking.

Per Serving: Calories: 510; Total Fat: 28g; Saturated Fat: 8g; Sodium: 440mg; Total Carbohydrates: 11g; Dietary Fiber: 0g; Total Sugars: 10g; Protein: 54g

Family Chicken Fingers

Servings: 4 | Prep Time: 10 Minutes | Cooking Time: 30 Minutes

Ingredients:

- 450g chicken breast fingers
- 1 tbsp chicken seasoning
- 1/2 tsp mustard powder
- Salt and pepper to taste
- 2 eggs
- 1 cup bread crumbs

Directions:

1. Preheat air fryer to 200°C/400°F.
2. Add the chicken fingers to a large bowl along with chicken seasoning, mustard, salt, and pepper; mix well.
3. Set up two small bowls. In one bowl, beat the eggs. In the second bowl, add the bread crumbs.
4. Dip the chicken in the egg, then dredge in breadcrumbs.
5. Place the nuggets in the air fryer. Lightly spray with cooking oil, then Air Fry for 8 minutes, shaking the basket once until crispy and cooked through.
6. Serve warm.

Variations & Ingredients Tips:

- Use panko breadcrumbs for extra crunch.
- Add grated parmesan to the breadcrumb mixture.
- Serve with your favorite dipping sauces like honey mustard or BBQ.

Per Serving: Calories: 290; Total Fat: 6g; Saturated Fat: 1.5g; Cholesterol: 180mg; Sodium: 480mg; Total Carbs: 16g; Dietary Fiber: 1g; Total Sugars: 1g; Protein: 40g

Cajun Chicken Livers

Servings: 2 | Prep Time: 30 Minutes (plus 2 Hours Marinating Time) | Cooking Time: 45 Minutes

Ingredients:

- 454 grams chicken livers, rinsed, connective tissue discarded
- 1 cup whole milk
- ½ cup cornmeal
- 3/4 cup flour
- 1 tsp salt and black pepper
- 1 tsp Cajun seasoning
- 2 eggs
- 1 ½ cups bread crumbs
- 1 tbsp olive oil
- 2 tbsp chopped parsley

Directions:

1. Pat chicken livers dry with paper towels, then transfer them to a small bowl and pour in the milk and black pepper. Let sit covered in the fridge for 2 hours.
2. Preheat air fryer at 190°C/375°F.
3. In a bowl, combine cornmeal, flour, salt, and Cajun seasoning. In another bowl, beat the eggs, and in a third bowl, add bread crumbs.
4. Dip chicken livers first in the cornmeal mixture, then in the egg, and finally in the bread crumbs.
5. Place chicken livers in the greased air fryer basket, brush the tops lightly with olive oil, and Air Fry for 16 minutes, turning once.
6. Serve right away sprinkled with parsley.

Variations & Ingredients Tips:

- Add a dash of hot sauce or cayenne pepper to the milk for extra spice.
- Serve with a side of remoulade sauce, hot sauce, or ranch dressing for dipping.
- Use a mixture of half cornmeal and half flour for a lighter coating.

Per Serving: Calories: 790; Total Fat: 30g; Saturated Fat: 9g; Sodium: 1530mg; Total Carbohydrates: 73g; Dietary Fiber: 4g; Total Sugars: 9g; Protein: 61g

Fish And Seafood Recipes

Shrimp

Servings: 4 | Prep Time: 5 Minutes | Cooking Time: 8 Minutes

Ingredients:

- 450g shrimp, peeled, deveined, and butterflied
- Marinade:
- 1 (150ml) can evaporated milk
- 2 eggs, beaten
- 2 tablespoons white vinegar
- 1 tablespoon baking powder
- Coating:
- 1 cup crushed panko breadcrumbs
- 1/2 teaspoon paprika
- 1/2 teaspoon Old Bay Seasoning
- 1/4 teaspoon garlic powder
- Oil for misting or cooking spray

Directions:

1. Make marinade and stir in shrimp to coat. Refrigerate 1 hour.
2. Preheat air fryer to 200°C/390°F.
3. Combine coating ingredients in a shallow dish.
4. Dip shrimp in marinade, then coat in crumb mixture. Spray with oil.
5. In two batches, place shrimp in a single layer in air fryer basket.
6. Cook at 200°C/390°F for 8 minutes until crispy and golden brown.

Variations & Ingredients Tips:

- Add hot sauce or cajun seasoning to the marinade.
- Substitute panko with crushed cornflakes or potato chips.
- Serve with lemon wedges, cocktail sauce or remoulade for dipping.

Per Serving: Calories: 270; Total Fat: 6g; Saturated Fat: 1g; Cholesterol: 225mg; Sodium: 760mg; Total Carbs: 26g; Dietary Fiber: 1g; Sugars: 4g; Protein: 26g

Salty German-style Shrimp Pancakes

Servings: 4 | Prep Time: 5 Minutes | Cooking Time: 15 Minutes

Ingredients:

- 1 tbsp butter
- 3 eggs, beaten
- 1/2 cup flour
- 1/2 cup milk
- 1/8 tsp salt
- 1 cup salsa
- 1 cup cooked shrimp, minced
- 2 tbsp cilantro, chopped

Directions:

1. Preheat air fryer to 200°C/390°F.
2. Mix the eggs, flour, milk, and salt in a bowl until frothy.
3. Pour the batter into a greased baking pan and place in the air fryer.
4. Bake for 15 minutes or until the pancake is puffed and golden.
5. Flip the pancake onto a plate.
6. Mix salsa, shrimp, and cilantro. Top the pancake and serve.

Variations & Ingredients Tips:

- Add diced onions, peppers or spinach to the batter.
- Use corn or whole wheat flour for extra nutrition.
- Serve with sour cream, guacamole or hot sauce.

Per Serving: Calories: 200; Total Fat: 7g; Saturated Fat: 3g; Cholesterol: 190mg; Sodium: 570mg; Total Carbs: 20g; Dietary Fiber: 2g; Sugars: 3g; Protein: 13g

Buttered Swordfish Steaks

Servings: 4 | Prep Time: 15 Minutes | Cooking Time: 30 Minutes

Ingredients:

- 4 swordfish steaks
- 2 eggs, beaten
- 85 grams melted butter
- ½ cup breadcrumbs
- Black pepper to taste
- 1 tsp dried rosemary
- 1 tsp dried marjoram
- 1 lemon, cut into wedges

Directions:

1. Preheat air fryer to 180°C/350°F.
2. Place the eggs and melted butter in a bowl and stir thoroughly.
3. Combine the breadcrumbs, rosemary, marjoram, and black pepper in a separate bowl.
4. Dip the swordfish steaks in the beaten eggs, then coat with the crumb mixture.
5. Place the coated fish in the air fryer basket.
6. Air Fry for 12-14 minutes, turning once until the fish is cooked through and the crust is toasted and crispy.
7. Serve with lemon wedges.

Variations & Ingredients Tips:

- Use cod, halibut, or mahi-mahi instead of swordfish for different fish options.
- Add grated Parmesan cheese or finely chopped nuts to the breading for extra flavor and texture.
- Serve with tartar sauce, garlic aioli, or a side of roasted vegetables.

Per Serving: Calories: 420; Total Fat: 27g; Saturated Fat: 15g; Sodium: 330mg; Total Carbohydrates: 11g; Dietary Fiber: 1g; Total Sugars: 1g; Protein: 33g

Crab Stuffed Salmon Roast

Servings: 4 | Prep Time: 15 Minutes | Cooking Time: 20 Minutes

Ingredients:

- 1 (680g) salmon fillet
- Salt and freshly ground black pepper
- 170g crabmeat
- 1 teaspoon finely chopped lemon zest
- 1 teaspoon Dijon mustard
- 1 tablespoon chopped fresh parsley, plus more for garnish
- 1 scallion, chopped
- 1/4 teaspoon salt
- Olive oil

Directions:

1. Prepare the salmon fillet by butterflying it. Slice into the thickest side of the salmon, parallel to the countertop and along the length of the fillet. Don't slice all the way through to the other side – stop about 2.5 cm from the edge. Open the salmon up like a book. Season the salmon with salt and freshly ground black pepper.
2. Make the crab filling by combining the crabmeat, lemon

36

zest, mustard, parsley, scallion, salt and freshly ground black pepper in a bowl. Spread this filling in the center of the salmon. Fold one side of the salmon over the filling. Then fold the other side over on top.
3. Transfer the rolled salmon to the center of a piece of parchment paper that is roughly 15 cm wide and about 30 cm long. The parchment paper will act as a sling, making it easier to put the salmon into the air fryer. Preheat the air fryer to 190°C/370°F. Use the parchment paper to transfer the salmon roast to the air fryer basket and tuck the ends of the paper down beside the salmon. Drizzle a little olive oil on top and season with salt and pepper.
4. Air-fry the salmon at 190°C/370°F for 20 minutes.
5. Remove the roast from the air fryer and let it rest for a few minutes. Then, slice it, sprinkle some more lemon zest and parsley (or fresh chives) on top and serve.

Variations & Ingredients Tips:

- Use a blend of crab and shrimp for the stuffing.
- Add some finely diced red bell pepper to the filling for color.
- Serve with lemon wedges and a side of roasted asparagus.

Per Serving: Calories: 330; Total Fat: 19g; Saturated Fat: 3.5g; Cholesterol: 115mg; Sodium: 490mg; Total Carbs: 2g; Dietary Fiber: 0g; Total Sugars: 1g; Protein: 36g

Breaded Parmesan Perch

Servings: 5 | Prep Time: 10 Minutes | Cooking Time: 15 Minutes

Ingredients:

- 1/4 cup grated Parmesan
- 1/2 tsp salt
- 1/4 tsp paprika
- 1 tbsp chopped dill
- 1 tsp dried thyme
- 2 tsp Dijon mustard
- 2 tbsp bread crumbs
- 4 ocean perch fillets
- 1 lemon, quartered
- 2 tbsp chopped cilantro

Directions:

1. Preheat air fryer to 200°C/400°F.
2. Combine salt, paprika, pepper, dill, mustard, thyme, Parmesan, and bread crumbs in a wide bowl.
3. Coat all sides of the fillets in the breading, then transfer to the greased frying basket.
4. Air Fry for 8 minutes until outside is golden and the inside is cooked through.
5. Garnish with lemon wedges and sprinkle with cilantro. Serve and enjoy!

Variations & Ingredients Tips:

- Use cod, haddock or flounder instead of perch.
- Add some lemon zest or garlic powder to the breading.
- Serve with a side of tartar sauce or marinara sauce.

Per Serving: Calories: 120; Total Fat: 4.5g; Saturated Fat: 1.5g; Cholesterol: 55mg; Sodium: 430mg; Total Carbs: 3g; Dietary Fiber: 0g; Total Sugars: 0g; Protein: 17g

Fish Nuggets With Broccoli Dip

Servings: 4 | Prep Time: 20 Minutes | Cooking Time: 40 Minutes

Ingredients:

- 450g cod fillets, cut into chunks
- 1 1/2 cups broccoli florets
- 1/4 cup grated Parmesan
- 3 garlic cloves, peeled
- 3 tbsp sour cream
- 2 tbsp lemon juice
- 2 tbsp olive oil
- 2 egg whites
- 1 cup panko bread crumbs
- 1 tsp dried dill
- Salt and pepper to taste

Directions:

1. Preheat the air fryer to 200°C/400°F.
2. Put the broccoli and garlic in the greased frying basket and Air Fry for 5-7 minutes or until tender. Remove to a blender and add sour cream, lemon juice, olive oil, and 1/2 tsp of salt and process until smooth. Set the sauce aside.
3. Beat the egg whites until frothy in a shallow bowl. On a plate, combine the panko, Parmesan, dill, pepper, and the remaining 1/2 tsp of salt.
4. Dip the cod fillets in the egg whites, then the breadcrumbs, pressing to coat. Put half the cubes in the frying basket and spray with cooking oil.
5. Air Fry for 6-8 minutes or until the fish is cooked through.
6. Serve the fish with the sauce and enjoy!

Variations & Ingredients Tips:

- Use salmon, pollack or tilapia instead of cod.
- Add some cayenne or smoked paprika to the breading for a kick.
- Serve with sweet potato fries and lemon wedges.

Per Serving: Calories: 350; Total Fat: 15g; Saturated Fat: 5g; Cholesterol: 85mg; Sodium: 540mg; Total Carbs: 22g; Dietary Fiber: 3g; Total Sugars: 3g; Protein: 34g

Mediterranean Salmon Cakes

Servings: 4 | Prep Time: 15 Minutes | Cooking Time: 30 Minutes

Ingredients:

- 1/4 cup heavy cream
- 5 tbsp mayonnaise
- 2 cloves garlic, minced
- 1/4 tsp caper juice
- 2 tsp lemon juice
- 1 tbsp capers
- 1 can salmon
- 2 tsp lemon zest
- 1 egg
- 1/4 minced red bell peppers
- 1/2 cup flour

- 1/8 tsp salt
- 2 tbsp sliced green olives

Directions:
1. Combine heavy cream, 2 tbsp mayonnaise, garlic, caper juices, capers, and lemon juice in a bowl. Place the resulting caper sauce in the fridge until ready to use.
2. Preheat air fryer to 200°C/400°F.
3. Combine canned salmon, lemon zest, egg, remaining mayonnaise, bell peppers, flour, and salt in a bowl. Form into 8 patties.
4. Place the patties in the greased frying basket and Air Fry for 10 minutes, turning once.
5. Let rest for 5 minutes before drizzling with lemon sauce. Garnish with green olives to serve.

Variations & Ingredients Tips:
- Use fresh salmon instead of canned.
- Add breadcrumbs or panko to the patty mixture to bind.
- Serve on a bed of greens or with roasted veggies.

Per Serving: Calories: 375; Total Fat: 27g; Saturated Fat: 6g; Cholesterol: 135mg; Sodium: 530mg; Total Carbs: 16g; Fiber: 1g; Sugars: 2g; Protein: 18g

Fish Tortillas With Coleslaw

Servings: 4 | Prep Time: 15 Minutes | Cooking Time: 30 Minutes

Ingredients:
- 1 tbsp olive oil
- 450g cod fillets
- 3 tbsp lemon juice
- 2 cups chopped red cabbage
- 1/2 cup salsa
- 1/3 cup sour cream
- 6 taco shells, warm
- 1 avocado, chopped

Directions:
1. Preheat air fryer to 200°C/400°F.
2. Brush oil on the cod and sprinkle with some lemon juice. Place in the frying basket and Air Fry until the fish flakes with a fork, 9-12 minutes.
3. Meanwhile, mix together the remaining lemon juice, red cabbage, salsa, and sour cream in a medium bowl.
4. Put the cooked fish in a bowl, breaking it into large pieces. Then add the cabbage mixture, avocados, and warmed tortilla shells ready for assembly.
5. Enjoy!

Variations & Ingredients Tips:
- Use tilapia, mahi mahi or catfish instead of cod.
- Add some chopped jalapeños or hot sauce to the slaw for a kick.
- Serve with lime wedges, cilantro and sliced radishes.

Per Serving: Calories: 370; Total Fat: 19g; Saturated Fat: 5g; Cholesterol: 75mg; Sodium: 620mg; Total Carbs: 27g; Dietary Fiber: 5g; Total Sugars: 4g; Protein: 29g

Sea Bass With Fruit Salsa

Servings: 4 | Prep Time: 15 Minutes | Cooking Time: 30 Minutes

Ingredients:
- 3 halved nectarines, pitted
- 4 sea bass fillets
- 2 tsp olive oil
- 3 plums, halved and pitted
- 1 cup red grapes
- 1 tbsp lemon juice
- 1 tbsp honey
- 1/2 tsp dried thyme

Directions:
1. Preheat air fryer to 200°C/390°F.
2. Lay sea bass fillets in frying basket, spritz with olive oil. Air Fry 4 minutes.
3. Remove basket, add nectarines, plums, grapes. Spritz with lemon juice, honey and thyme.
4. Return basket to fryer and Bake 5-9 more minutes until fish flakes and fruit is soft.
5. Serve hot.

Variations & Ingredients Tips:
- Use other fruits like pineapple, mango or strawberries.
- Add jalapeño or red onion to the salsa.
- Squeeze lime juice over the top before serving.

Per Serving: Calories: 220; Total Fat: 4g; Saturated Fat: 1g; Cholesterol: 65mg; Sodium: 65mg; Total Carbs: 25g; Dietary Fiber: 3g; Sugars: 18g; Protein: 22g

Hot Calamari Rings

Servings: 4 | Prep Time: 15 Minutes | Cooking Time: 25 Minutes

Ingredients:
- 1/2 cup all-purpose flour
- 2 tsp hot chili powder
- 2 eggs
- 1 tbsp milk
- 1 cup bread crumbs
- Salt and pepper to taste
- 450g calamari rings
- 1 lime, quartered
- 1/2 cup aioli sauce

Directions:
1. Preheat air fryer at 200°C/400°F.
2. In one bowl, mix flour and chili powder.
3. In another bowl, whisk eggs and milk.
4. In a third bowl, mix breadcrumbs, salt and pepper.
5. Dredge calamari in flour, then egg, then breadcrumbs to coat.

6. Place in greased air fryer basket and cook for 4 mins, tossing once.
7. Squeeze lime over calamari and serve with aioli sauce.

Variations & Ingredients Tips:

- Add parmesan or lemon zest to the breadcrumb mixture.
- Use panko breadcrumbs for extra crunch.
- Serve with marinara sauce instead of aioli.

Per Serving: Calories: 283; Total Fat: 10g; Saturated Fat: 2g; Cholesterol: 188mg; Sodium: 540mg; Total Carbs: 29g; Dietary Fiber: 1g; Total Sugars: 2g; Protein: 19g

Caribbean Jerk Cod Fillets

Servings: 2 | Prep Time: 10 Minutes | Cooking Time: 20 Minutes

Ingredients:

- ¼ cup chopped cooked shrimp
- ¼ cup diced mango
- 1 tomato, diced
- 2 tbsp diced red onion
- 1 tbsp chopped parsley
- ¼ tsp ginger powder
- 2 tsp lime juice
- Salt and pepper to taste
- 2 cod fillets
- 2 tsp Jerk seasoning

Directions:

1. In a bowl, combine the shrimp, mango, tomato, red onion, parsley, ginger powder, lime juice, salt, and black pepper. Let chill the salsa in the fridge until ready to use.
2. Preheat air fryer to 180°C/350°F.
3. Sprinkle cod fillets with Jerk seasoning. Place them in the greased air fryer basket and Air Fry for 10 minutes or until the cod is opaque and flakes easily with a fork.
4. Divide between 2 medium plates. Serve topped with the Caribbean salsa.

Variations & Ingredients Tips:

- Substitute cod with halibut, mahi-mahi, or snapper fillets.
- Use pineapple or papaya instead of mango for a different tropical flavor.
- Add a dash of hot sauce or minced jalapeño to the salsa for extra heat.

Per Serving: Calories: 200; Total Fat: 2g; Saturated Fat: 0g; Sodium: 530mg; Total Carbohydrates: 14g; Dietary Fiber: 2g; Total Sugars: 9g; Protein: 32g

Stuffed Shrimp

Servings: 4 | Prep Time: 25 Minutes | Cooking Time: 12 Minutes Per Batch

Ingredients:

- 16 tail-on shrimp, peeled and deveined (last tail section intact)
- 3/4 cup crushed panko breadcrumbs
- Oil for misting or cooking spray
- Stuffing:
- 2 (170g) cans lump crabmeat
- 2 tablespoons chopped shallots
- 2 tablespoons chopped green onions
- 2 tablespoons chopped celery
- 2 tablespoons chopped green bell pepper
- 1/2 cup crushed saltine crackers
- 1 teaspoon Old Bay Seasoning
- 1 teaspoon garlic powder
- 1/4 teaspoon ground thyme
- 2 teaspoons dried parsley flakes
- 2 teaspoons fresh lemon juice
- 2 teaspoons Worcestershire sauce
- 1 egg, beaten

Directions:

1. Rinse shrimp. Remove tail section (shell) from 4 shrimp, discard, and chop the meat finely.
2. To prepare the remaining 12 shrimp, cut a deep slit down the back side so that the meat lies open flat. Do not cut all the way through.
3. Preheat air fryer to 180°C/360°F.
4. Place chopped shrimp in a large bowl with all of the stuffing ingredients and stir to combine.
5. Divide stuffing into 12 portions, about 2 tablespoons each.
6. Place one stuffing portion onto the back of each shrimp and form into a ball or oblong shape. Press firmly so that stuffing sticks together and adheres to shrimp.
7. Gently roll each stuffed shrimp in panko crumbs and mist with oil or cooking spray.
8. Place 6 shrimp in air fryer basket and cook at 180°C/360°F for 10 minutes. Mist with oil or spray and cook 2 minutes longer or until stuffing cooks through inside and is crispy outside.
9. Repeat step 8 to cook remaining shrimp.

Variations & Ingredients Tips:

- Substitute crab with cooked lobster, salmon or firm white fish.
- Add some diced jalapeño or red pepper flakes to the stuffing for heat.
- Serve with lemon wedges and a remoulade or cocktail sauce for dipping.

Per Serving: Calories: 290; Total Fat: 8g; Saturated Fat: 1.5g; Cholesterol: 230mg; Sodium: 940mg; Total Carbs: 19g; Dietary Fiber: 1g; Total Sugars: 2g; Protein: 34g

Halibut With Coleslaw

Servings: 4 | Prep Time: 15 Minutes | Cooking Time: 30 Minutes

Ingredients:

- 1 bag coleslaw mix
- 1/4 cup mayonnaise
- 1 tsp lemon zest
- 1 tbsp lemon juice
- 1 shredded carrot
- 1/2 cup buttermilk
- 1 tsp grated onion
- 4 halibut fillets
- Salt and pepper to taste

Directions:

1. Combine coleslaw mix, mayonnaise, carrot, buttermilk, onion, lemon zest, lemon juice, and salt in a bowl. Let chill the coleslaw covered in the fridge until ready to use.
2. Preheat air fryer at 175°C/350°F.
3. Sprinkle halibut with salt and pepper. Place them in the greased frying basket and Air Fry for 10 minutes until the fillets are opaque and flake easily with a fork.
4. Serve with chilled coleslaw.

Variations & Ingredients Tips:

- Add some chopped apples, raisins or pineapple to the coleslaw.
- Use Greek yogurt instead of mayo for a lighter dressing.
- Serve the fish and slaw in tacos, wraps or sliders.

Per Serving: Calories: 290; Total Fat: 10g; Saturated Fat: 2.5g; Cholesterol: 100mg; Sodium: 460mg; Total Carbs: 13g; Dietary Fiber: 2g; Total Sugars: 6g; Protein: 36g

Restaurant-style Breaded Shrimp

Servings: 2 | Prep Time: 15 Minutes | Cooking Time: 35 Minutes

Ingredients:

- 225g fresh shrimp, peeled
- 2 eggs, beaten
- 1/2 cup breadcrumbs
- 1/2 onion, finely chopped
- 1/2 tsp ground ginger
- 1/2 tsp garlic powder
- 1/2 tsp turmeric
- 1/2 tsp red chili powder
- Salt and pepper to taste
- 1/2 tsp amchur powder

Directions:

1. Preheat air fryer to 175°C/350°F.
2. Place beaten eggs in a bowl and dip in the shrimp.
3. Blend breadcrumbs with all the dry ingredients in another bowl.
4. Add shrimp and toss to coat.
5. Place coated shrimp in greased frying basket.
6. Air Fry 12-14 minutes until crust is golden brown, tossing 2-3 times.
7. Serve.

Variations & Ingredients Tips:

- Use panko breadcrumbs for extra crunch.
- Add cajun or old bay seasoning to the coating.
- Serve with cocktail sauce, lemon wedges or remoulade.

Per Serving: Calories: 295; Total Fat: 6g; Saturated Fat: 2g; Cholesterol: 285mg; Sodium: 700mg; Total Carbs: 34g; Dietary Fiber: 2g; Sugars: 3g; Protein: 27g

Five Spice Red Snapper With Green Onions And Orange Salsa

Servings: 2 | Prep Time: 15 Minutes | Cooking Time: 8 Minutes

Ingredients:

- 2 oranges, peeled, segmented and chopped
- 1 tablespoon minced shallot
- 1 to 3 teaspoons minced red jalapeño or serrano pepper
- 1 tablespoon chopped fresh cilantro
- Lime juice, to taste
- Salt, to taste
- 2 (140 to 170g) red snapper fillets
- 1/2 teaspoon Chinese five spice powder
- Salt and freshly ground black pepper
- Vegetable or olive oil, in a spray bottle
- 4 green onions, cut into 5-cm lengths

Directions:

1. Start by making the salsa. Cut the peel off the oranges, slicing around the oranges to expose the flesh. Segment the oranges by cutting in between the membranes of the orange. Chop the segments roughly and combine in a bowl with the shallot, jalapeño or serrano pepper, cilantro, lime juice and salt. Set the salsa aside.
2. Preheat the air fryer to 200°C/400°F.
3. Season the fish fillets with the five-spice powder, salt and freshly ground black pepper. Spray both sides of the fish fillets with oil. Toss the green onions with a little oil.
4. Transfer the fish to the air fryer basket and scatter the green onions around the fish. Air-fry at 200°C/400°F for 8 minutes.
5. Remove the fish from the air fryer, along with the fried green onions. Serve with white rice and a spoonful of the salsa on top.

Variations & Ingredients Tips:

- Use cod, tilapia or mahi mahi instead of red snapper.
- Add some diced mango or pineapple to the salsa.
- Serve over rice noodles or stir-fried vegetables.

Per Serving: Calories: 250; Total Fat: 5g; Saturated Fat: 1g; Cholesterol: 60mg; Sodium: 140mg; Total Carbs: 20g; Dietary Fiber: 4g; Total Sugars: 13g; Protein: 32g

Honey Pecan Shrimp

Servings: 4 | Prep Time: 15 Minutes | Cooking

Time: 10 Minutes

Ingredients:

- 1/4 cup cornstarch
- 3/4 teaspoon sea salt, divided
- 1/4 teaspoon pepper
- 2 egg whites
- 2/3 cup finely chopped pecans
- 450g raw, peeled, and deveined shrimp
- 1/4 cup honey
- 2 tablespoons mayonnaise

Directions:

1. In a small bowl, whisk together the cornstarch, 1/2 teaspoon of the salt, and the pepper.
2. In a second bowl, whisk together the egg whites until soft and foamy. (They don't need to be whipped to peaks or even soft peaks, just frothy.)
3. In a third bowl, mix together the pecans and the remaining 1/4 teaspoon of sea salt.
4. Pat the shrimp dry with paper towels. Working in small batches, dip the shrimp into the cornstarch, then into the egg whites, and then into the pecans until all the shrimp are coated with pecans.
5. Preheat the air fryer to 165°C/330°F.
6. Place the coated shrimp inside the air fryer basket and spray with cooking spray. Cook for 5 minutes, toss the shrimp, and cook another 5 minutes.
7. Meanwhile, place the honey in a microwave-safe bowl and microwave for 30 seconds. Whisk in the mayonnaise until smooth and creamy. Pour the honey sauce into a serving bowl. Add the cooked shrimp to the serving bowl while hot and toss to coat.
8. Serve immediately.

Variations & Ingredients Tips:

- Use walnuts, almonds or panko instead of pecans.
- Add some cayenne or chili powder to the cornstarch for heat.
- Serve over a bed of greens with a citrus vinaigrette.

Per Serving: Calories: 390; Total Fat: 21g; Saturated Fat: 2g; Cholesterol: 230mg; Sodium: 990mg; Total Carbs: 29g; Dietary Fiber: 1g; Total Sugars: 20g; Protein: 27g

Aromatic Ahi Tuna Steaks

Servings: 4 | Prep Time: 5 Minutes | Cooking Time: 15 Minutes

Ingredients:

- 1 tsp garlic powder
- 1/2 tsp salt
- 1/4 tsp dried thyme
- 1/4 tsp dried oregano
- 1/4 tsp cayenne pepper
- 4 ahi tuna steaks
- 2 tbsp olive oil
- 1 lemon, cut into wedges

Directions:

1. Preheat air fryer to 190°C/380°F.
2. Stir together the garlic powder, salt, thyme, cayenne pepper and oregano in a bowl to combine.
3. Coat the tuna steaks with olive oil. Season both sides of each steak with the seasoning mix.
4. Put the steaks in the frying basket. Air Fry for 5 minutes, then flip and cook for an additional 3-4 minutes.
5. Serve warm with lemon wedges on the side.

Variations & Ingredients Tips:

- Use salmon, swordfish or mahi mahi instead of tuna.
- Add a sprinkle of sesame seeds before air frying.
- Serve over a bed of salad greens or rice.

Per Serving: Calories: 220; Total Fat: 8g; Saturated Fat: 1.5g; Cholesterol: 65mg; Sodium: 380mg; Total Carbs: 1g; Dietary Fiber: 0g; Total Sugars: 0g; Protein: 34g

Lobster Tails With Lemon Garlic Butter

Servings: 2 | Prep Time: 10 Minutes | Cooking Time: 5 Minutes

Ingredients:

- 115-g unsalted butter
- 1 tablespoon finely chopped lemon zest
- 1 clove garlic, thinly sliced
- 2 (170-g) lobster tails
- Salt and freshly ground black pepper
- 1/2 cup white wine
- 1/2 lemon, sliced
- Vegetable oil

Directions:

1. Make the lemon garlic butter by combining butter, lemon zest and garlic in a saucepan. Melt and simmer over low heat while preparing the lobster.
2. Cut down the top shell of each lobster tail. Crack the bottom shell so you can access the meat inside. Pull meat up out of shell, leaving it attached at the base.
3. Lay meat over shell and season with salt and pepper. Pour some lemon garlic butter over meat and refrigerate briefly to solidify butter.
4. Pour white wine into air fryer drawer and add lemon slices. Preheat to 200°C/400°F for 5 mins.
5. Transfer lobsters to air fryer basket. Air-fry at 190°C/370°F for 5 mins, brushing more butter on halfway through. (Add 1-2 mins if tails are over 170-g.)
6. Serve with remaining butter for dipping.

Variations & Ingredients Tips:

- Add dried herbs like thyme or parsley to the butter.
- Stuff the tail cavity with breadcrumbs before cooking.
- Squeeze lemon juice over lobster before serving.

Per Serving: Calories: 550; Total Fat: 45g; Saturated Fat: 28g; Cholesterol: 140mg; Sodium: 600mg; Total Carbs: 6g; Dietary Fiber: 0g; Total Sugars: 1g; Protein: 22g

Sea Bass With Potato Scales And Caper Aïoli

Servings: 2 | Prep Time: 10 Minutes | Cooking Time: 10 Minutes

Ingredients:

- 2 (170-225g) fillets of sea bass
- Salt and freshly ground black pepper
- 1/4 cup mayonnaise
- 2 teaspoons finely chopped lemon zest
- 1 teaspoon chopped fresh thyme
- 2 fingerling potatoes, very thinly sliced into rounds
- Olive oil
- 1/2 clove garlic, crushed into a paste
- 1 tablespoon capers, drained and rinsed
- 1 tablespoon olive oil
- 1 teaspoon lemon juice, to taste

Directions:

1. Preheat air fryer to 200°C/400°F.
2. Season fish with salt and pepper. Mix mayo, zest and thyme. Spread thin layer on fillets.
3. Layer overlapping potato slices on fish to resemble scales, pressing to adhere. Season with salt and brush with oil.
4. Air-fry fish for 8-10 mins, until potatoes are crisp.
5. Make aioli by mixing remaining mayo with garlic, capers, oil and lemon juice.
6. Serve fish warm with aioli dolloped on top.

Variations & Ingredients Tips:

- Try other white fish like halibut or cod.
- Use sweet potatoes instead of regular for the "scales".
- Add fresh herbs like dill or parsley to the aioli.

Per Serving: Calories: 450; Total Fat: 32g; Saturated Fat: 5g; Cholesterol: 65mg; Sodium: 590mg; Total Carbs: 22g; Dietary Fiber: 2g; Sugars: 1g; Protein: 21g

Mediterranean Cod Croquettes

Servings: 4 | Prep Time: 20 Minutes | Cooking Time: 30 Minutes

Ingredients:

- 1/2 cup instant mashed potatoes
- 340g raw cod fillet, flaked
- 2 large eggs, beaten
- 1/4 cup sour cream
- 2 tsp olive oil
- 1/3 cup chopped thyme
- 1 shallot, minced
- 1 garlic clove, minced
- 1 cup bread crumbs
- 1 tsp lemon juice
- Salt and pepper to taste
- 1/2 tsp dried basil
- 5 tbsp Greek yogurt
- 1/2 tsp harissa paste
- 1 tbsp chopped dill

Directions:

1. In a bowl, combine the fish, 1 egg, sour cream, instant mashed potatoes, olive oil, thyme, shallot, garlic, 2 tbsp of the bread crumbs, salt, dill, lemon juice, and pepper; mix well. Refrigerate for 30 minutes.
2. Mix yogurt, harissa paste, and basil in a bowl until blended. Set aside.
3. Preheat air fryer to 175°C/350°F.
4. Take the fish mixture out of the refrigerator. Knead and shape the mixture into 12 logs.
5. In a bowl, place the remaining egg. In a second bowl, add the remaining bread crumbs.
6. Dip the croquettes into the egg and shake off the excess drips. Then roll the logs into the breadcrumbs.
7. Place the croquettes in the greased frying basket. Air Fry for 10 minutes, flipping once until golden.
8. Serve with the yogurt sauce.

Variations & Ingredients Tips:

- Use other white fish like haddock or pollock.
- Add shredded cheese like parmesan to the croquette mixture.
- Serve with lemon wedges.

Per Serving: Calories: 355, Total Fat: 9g, Saturated Fat: 3g, Cholesterol: 135mg, Sodium: 510mg, Total Carbs: 41g, Fiber: 2g, Sugars: 3g, Protein: 26g

Horseradish Crusted Salmon

Servings: 2 | Prep Time: 10 Minutes | Cooking Time: 14 Minutes

Ingredients:

- 2 (140g) salmon fillets
- Salt and freshly ground black pepper
- 2 teaspoons Dijon mustard
- 1/2 cup panko breadcrumbs
- 2 tablespoons prepared horseradish
- 1/2 teaspoon finely chopped lemon zest
- 1 tablespoon olive oil
- 1 tablespoon chopped fresh parsley

Directions:

1. Preheat the air fryer to 180°C/360°F.
2. Season the salmon with salt and freshly ground black pepper. Then spread the Dijon mustard on the salmon, coating the entire surface.
3. Combine the breadcrumbs, horseradish, lemon zest and olive oil in a small bowl. Spread the mixture over the top of the salmon and press down lightly with your hands, adhering it to the salmon using the mustard as "glue".
4. Transfer the salmon to the air fryer basket and air-fry at 180°C/360°F for 14 minutes (depending on how thick your fillet is) or until the fish feels firm to the touch.
5. Sprinkle with the parsley.

Variations & Ingredients Tips:

- Use Dijon or whole grain mustard for a milder flavor.
- Add some grated parmesan or asiago to the breadcrumb mixture.
- Serve over a bed of sautéed spinach or roasted asparagus.

Per Serving: Calories: 400; Total Fat: 24g; Saturated Fat: 4g; Cholesterol: 85mg; Sodium: 500mg; Total Carbs: 13g; Dietary Fiber: 1g; Total Sugars: 1g; Protein: 34g

Maple-crusted Salmon

Servings: 2 | Prep Time: 35 Minutes (includes Marinating) | Cooking Time: 8 Minutes

Ingredients:

- 340g salmon filets
- 1/3 cup maple syrup
- 1 teaspoon Worcestershire sauce
- 2 teaspoons Dijon mustard or brown mustard
- 1/2 cup finely chopped walnuts
- 1/2 teaspoon sea salt
- 1/2 lemon
- 1 tablespoon chopped parsley, for garnish

Directions:

1. Place the salmon in a shallow baking dish. Top with maple syrup, Worcestershire sauce, and mustard. Refrigerate for 30 minutes.
2. Preheat the air fryer to 175°C/350°F.
3. Remove the salmon from the marinade and discard the marinade.
4. Place the chopped nuts on top of the salmon filets, and sprinkle salt on top of the nuts. Place the salmon, skin side down, in the air fryer basket. Cook for 6 to 8 minutes or until the fish flakes in the center.
5. Remove the salmon and plate on a serving platter. Squeeze fresh lemon over the top of the salmon and top with chopped parsley. Serve immediately.

Variations & Ingredients Tips:

- Use other nuts like pecans or almonds instead of walnuts.
- Brush with additional maple syrup after cooking for extra glaze.
- Serve with roasted vegetables or a fresh salad.

Per Serving: Calories: 550; Total Fat: 33g; Saturated Fat: 5g; Cholesterol: 105mg; Sodium: 420mg; Total Carbs: 26g; Dietary Fiber: 2g; Total Sugars: 18g; Protein: 36g

Mojito Fish Tacos

Servings: 4 | Prep Time: 15 Minutes | Cooking Time: 30 Minutes

Ingredients:

- 1 1/2 cups chopped red cabbage
- 450g cod fillets
- 2 tsp olive oil
- 3 tbsp lemon juice
- 1 large carrot, grated
- 1 tbsp white rum
- 1/2 cup salsa
- 1/3 cup Greek yogurt
- 4 soft tortillas

Directions:

1. Preheat air fryer to 200°C/390°F.
2. Rub the fish with olive oil, then a splash with 1 tbsp of lemon juice.
3. Place in the fryer and Air Fry for 9-12 minutes. The fish should flake when done.
4. Mix the remaining 2 tbsp lemon juice, red cabbage, carrots, salsa, rum, and yogurt in a bowl.
5. Take the fish out of the fryer and tear into large pieces.
6. Serve with tortillas and cabbage mixture. Enjoy!

Variations & Ingredients Tips:

- Use other white fish like tilapia or mahi mahi.
- Add diced mango or pineapple to the cabbage slaw.
- Drizzle with extra lime juice and chopped cilantro.

Per Serving: Calories: 255; Total Fat: 4g; Saturated Fat: 1g; Cholesterol: 60mg; Sodium: 360mg; Total Carbs: 25g; Fiber: 3g; Sugars: 6g; Protein: 29g

Tex-mex Fish Tacos

Servings: 3 | Prep Time: 10 Minutes | Cooking Time: 7 Minutes

Ingredients:

- ¾ tsp chile powder
- ¼ tsp ground cumin
- ¼ tsp dried oregano
- 3 140g skinless mahi-mahi fillets
- Vegetable oil spray
- 3 corn or flour tortillas
- 6 tbsp diced tomatoes
- 3 tbsp regular, low-fat, or fat-free sour cream

Directions:

1. Preheat the air fryer to 200°C/400°F.
2. Stir the chile powder, cumin, and oregano in a small bowl until well combined.
3. Coat each piece of fish all over (even the sides and ends) with vegetable oil spray. Sprinkle the spice mixture evenly over all sides of the fillets. Lightly spray them again.
4. When the machine is at temperature, set the fillets in the basket with as much air space between them as possible. Air-fry undisturbed for 7 minutes, until lightly browned and firm but not hard.
5. Use a nonstick-safe spatula to transfer the fillets to a wire rack. Microwave the tortillas on high for a few seconds, until supple. Put a fillet in each tortilla and top each with 2 tbsp diced tomatoes and 1 tbsp sour cream.

Variations & Ingredients Tips:

- Use cod, tilapia or catfish instead of mahi-mahi.
- Add some shredded cabbage or lettuce for crunch.

- Top with avocado slices or guacamole for creamy richness.

Per Serving: Calories: 230; Total Fat: 5g; Saturated Fat: 1.5g; Cholesterol: 90mg; Sodium: 280mg; Total Carbohydrates: 15g; Dietary Fiber: 2g; Total Sugars: 2g; Protein: 31g

Horseradish Tuna Croquettes

Servings: 4 | Prep Time: 20 Minutes | Cooking Time: 40 Minutes

Ingredients:

- 1 can tuna in water, drained
- 1/3 cup mayonnaise
- 1 tbsp minced celery
- 1 green onion, sliced
- 2 tsp dried dill
- 1 tsp lime juice
- 1 cup bread crumbs
- 1 egg
- 1 tsp prepared horseradish

Directions:

1. Preheat air fryer to 190°C/370°F.
2. Add the tuna, mayonnaise, celery, green onion, dill, lime juice, 1/4 cup bread crumbs, egg, and horseradish in a bowl and mix to combine.
3. Mold the mixture into 12 rectangular mound shapes. Roll each croquette in a shallow dish with 3/4 cup of bread crumbs.
4. Place croquettes in the lightly greased frying basket and Air Fry for 12 minutes on all sides.
5. Serve.

Variations & Ingredients Tips:

- Use canned salmon or crab meat instead of tuna.
- Add some capers, lemon zest or Old Bay seasoning to the mix.
- Serve with a creamy dill sauce or tartar sauce.

Per Serving: Calories: 320; Total Fat: 20g; Saturated Fat: 3.5g; Cholesterol: 80mg; Sodium: 510mg; Total Carbs: 20g; Dietary Fiber: 1g; Total Sugars: 2g; Protein: 18g

Firecracker Popcorn Shrimp

Servings: 6 | Prep Time: 20 Minutes | Cooking Time: 8 Minutes

Ingredients:

- 1/2 cup all-purpose flour
- 2 teaspoons ground paprika
- 1 teaspoon garlic powder
- 1/2 teaspoon black pepper
- 1/4 teaspoon salt
- 2 eggs, whisked
- 1 1/2 cups panko breadcrumbs
- 450g small shrimp, peeled and deveined

Directions:

1. Preheat the air fryer to 180°C/360°F.
2. In a medium bowl, place the flour and mix in the paprika, garlic powder, pepper, and salt.
3. In a shallow dish, place the eggs.
4. In a third dish, place the breadcrumbs.
5. Assemble the shrimp by covering them in the flour, then dipping them into the egg, and then coating them with the breadcrumbs. Repeat until all the shrimp are covered in the breading.
6. Liberally spray the metal trivet that fits in the air fryer basket with olive oil mist. Place the shrimp onto the trivet, leaving space between the shrimp to flip. Cook for 4 minutes, flip the shrimp, and cook another 4 minutes. Repeat until all the shrimp are cooked.
7. Serve warm with desired dipping sauce.

Variations & Ingredients Tips:

- Add some cayenne or red pepper flakes to the flour for extra heat.
- Substitute panko with crushed tortilla chips or corn flakes.
- Serve in tacos with cabbage slaw and avocado crema.

Per Serving: Calories: 240; Total Fat: 5g; Saturated Fat: 1g; Cholesterol: 185mg; Sodium: 560mg; Total Carbs: 26g; Dietary Fiber: 1g; Total Sugars: 1g; Protein: 21g

Garlic-lemon Steamer Clams

Servings: 2 | Prep Time: 25 Minutes | Cooking Time: 30 Minutes

Ingredients:

- 25 Manila clams, scrubbed
- 2 tbsp butter, melted
- 1 garlic clove, minced
- 2 lemon wedges

Directions:

1. Add the clams to a large bowl filled with water and let sit for 10 minutes. Drain. Pour more water and let sit for 10 more minutes. Drain.
2. Preheat air fryer to 175°C/350°F. Place clams in the basket and Air Fry for 7 minutes. Discard any clams that don't open.
3. Remove clams from shells and place them into a large serving dish. Drizzle with melted butter and garlic and squeeze lemon on top.
4. Serve.

Variations & Ingredients Tips:

- Add some white wine, shallots or parsley to the butter sauce.
- Use littleneck or cherrystone clams instead of Manila.
- Serve with crusty bread for dipping in the sauce.

44

Per Serving: Calories: 270; Total Fat: 15g; Saturated Fat: 8g; Cholesterol: 75mg; Sodium: 180mg; Total Carbs: 9g; Dietary Fiber: 0g; Total Sugars: 0g; Protein: 25g

Peanut-crusted Salmon

Servings: 4 | Prep Time: 15 Minutes | Cooking Time: 30 Minutes

Ingredients:

- 4 salmon fillets
- 2 eggs, beaten
- 85g melted butter
- 1 garlic clove, minced
- 1 tsp lemon zest
- 1 lemon
- 1 tsp celery salt
- 1 tbsp parsley, chopped
- 1 tsp dill, chopped
- 1/2 cup peanuts, crushed

Directions:

1. Preheat air fryer to 175°C/350°F.
2. Put the beaten eggs, melted butter, lemon juice, lemon zest, garlic, parsley, celery salt, and dill in a bowl and stir thoroughly.
3. Dip in the salmon fillets, then roll them in the crushed peanuts, coating completely.
4. Place the coated salmon fillets in the frying basket.
5. Air Fry for 14-16 minutes, flipping once halfway through cooking, until the salmon is cooked through and the crust is toasted and crispy.
6. Serve.

Variations & Ingredients Tips:

- Use other nuts like almonds or pecans instead of peanuts.
- Add cayenne or chili powder to the coating for some heat.
- Serve over a salad or with roasted vegetables.

Per Serving: Calories: 550; Total Fat: 40g; Saturated Fat: 12g; Cholesterol: 180mg; Sodium: 450mg; Total Carbs: 14g; Dietary Fiber: 2g; Sugars: 2g; Protein: 35g

Crispy Sweet-and-sour Cod Fillets

Servings: 3 | Prep Time: 10 Minutes | Cooking Time: 12 Minutes

Ingredients:

- 1 1/2 cups plain panko bread crumbs (gluten-free, if a concern)
- 2 tablespoons regular or low-fat mayonnaise (not fat-free; gluten-free, if a concern)
- 1/4 cup sweet pickle relish
- 3 (115 to 140g) skinless cod fillets

Directions:

1. Preheat the air fryer to 200°C/400°F.
2. Pour the bread crumbs into a shallow soup plate or a small pie plate.
3. Mix the mayonnaise and relish in a small bowl until well combined. Smear this mixture all over the cod fillets. Set them in the crumbs and turn until evenly coated on all sides, even on the ends.
4. Set the coated cod fillets in the basket with as much air space between them as possible. They should not touch. Air-fry undisturbed for 12 minutes, or until browned and crisp.
5. Use a nonstick-safe spatula to transfer the cod pieces to a wire rack. Cool for only a minute or two before serving hot.

Variations & Ingredients Tips:

- Use tilapia, basa or catfish instead of cod.
- Substitute pickle relish with sweet chili sauce or mango chutney.
- Sprinkle with chopped scallions and toasted sesame seeds before serving.

Per Serving: Calories: 280; Total Fat: 8g; Saturated Fat: 1.5g; Cholesterol: 85mg; Sodium: 630mg; Total Carbs: 24g; Dietary Fiber: 1g; Total Sugars: 5g; Protein: 27g

Creole Tilapia With Garlic Mayo

Servings: 4 | Prep Time: 10 Minutes | Cooking Time: 20 Minutes

Ingredients:

- 4 tilapia fillets
- 2 tbsp olive oil
- 1 tsp paprika
- 1 tsp garlic powder
- 1 tsp dried basil
- 1/2 tsp Creole seasoning
- 1/2 tsp chili powder
- 2 garlic cloves, minced
- 1 tbsp mayonnaise
- 1 tsp olive oil
- 1/2 lemon, juiced
- Salt and pepper to taste

Directions:

1. Preheat air fryer to 200°C/400°F.
2. Coat the tilapia with some olive oil, then season with paprika, garlic powder, basil, and Creole seasoning.
3. Bake in the greased frying basket for 15 minutes, flipping once during cooking.
4. While the fish is cooking, whisk together garlic, mayonnaise, olive oil, lemon juice, chili powder, salt and pepper in a bowl.
5. Serve the cooked fish with the aioli.

Variations & Ingredients Tips:

- Use catfish, cod or snapper instead of tilapia.
- Add some diced tomatoes and green onions to the mayo for a remoulade.
- Serve over a bed of dirty rice or Cajun-style coleslaw.

Per Serving: Calories: 240; Total Fat: 13g; Saturated Fat: 2g; Cholesterol: 85mg; Sodium: 260mg; Total Carbs: 2g; Dietary

Fiber: 0g; Total Sugars: 0g; Protein: 30g

Beef, Pork & Lamb Recipes

Tandoori Lamb Samosas

Servings: 2 | Prep Time: 15 Minutes | Cooking Time: 20 Minutes

Ingredients:

- 170 g ground lamb, sautéed
- 59 g spinach, torn
- ½ onion, minced
- 1 teaspoon tandoori masala
- ½ teaspoon ginger-garlic paste
- ½ teaspoon red chili powder
- ½ teaspoon turmeric powder
- Salt and pepper to taste
- 3 puff dough sheets

Directions:

1. Preheat air fryer to 175°C/350°F. Put the ground lamb, tandoori masala, ginger garlic paste, red chili powder, turmeric powder, salt, and pepper in a bowl and stir to combine. Add in the spinach and onion and stir until the ingredients are evenly blended. Divide the mixture into three equal segments.
2. Lay the pastry dough sheets out on a lightly floured surface. Fill each sheet of dough with one of the three portions of lamb mix, then fold the pastry over into a triangle, sealing the edges with a bit of water. Transfer the samosas to the greased frying basket and Air Fry for 12 minutes, flipping once until the samosas are crispy and flaky. Remove and leave to cool for 5 minutes. Serve.

Variations & Ingredients Tips:

- Use ground beef, chicken or potatoes instead of lamb
- Add some peas, carrots or cauliflower to the filling
- Serve with mint chutney or tamarind sauce for dipping

Per Serving: Calories: 548; Total Fat: 39g; Saturated Fat: 15g; Cholesterol: 86mg; Sodium: 383mg; Total Carbs: 28g; Dietary Fiber: 2g; Total Sugars: 1g; Protein: 25g

T-bone Steak With Roasted Tomato, Corn And Asparagus Salsa

Servings: 2 | Prep Time: 10 Minutes | Cooking Time: 15-20 Minutes

Ingredients:

- 1 (567g) T-bone steak
- Salt and freshly ground black pepper
- Salsa
- 1 1/2 cups cherry tomatoes
- 3/4 cup corn kernels (fresh, or frozen and thawed)
- 1 1/2 cups sliced asparagus (2.5cm slices) (about 1/2 bunch)
- 1 tablespoon + 1 teaspoon olive oil, divided
- Salt and freshly ground black pepper
- 1 1/2 teaspoons red wine vinegar
- 3 tablespoons chopped fresh basil
- 1 tablespoon chopped fresh chives

Directions:

1. Preheat the air fryer to 400°F/205°C.
2. Season the steak with salt and pepper and air-fry at 400°F/205°C for 10 minutes (medium-rare), 12 minutes (medium), or 15 minutes (well-done), flipping the steak once halfway through the cooking time.
3. In the meantime, toss the tomatoes, corn and asparagus in a bowl with a teaspoon or so of olive oil, salt and freshly ground black pepper.
4. When the steak has finished cooking, remove it to a cutting board, tent loosely with foil and let it rest. Transfer the vegetables to the air fryer and air-fry at 400°F/205°C for 5 minutes, shaking the basket once or twice during the cooking process.
5. Transfer the cooked vegetables back into the bowl and toss with the red wine vinegar, remaining olive oil and fresh herbs.
6. To serve, slice the steak on the bias and serve with some of the salsa on top.

Variations & Ingredients Tips:

- Use different colored cherry tomatoes for a pop of color
- Substitute zucchini or bell peppers for the asparagus
- Add a squeeze of lemon juice to the salsa for extra brightness

Per Serving: Calories: 630; Total Fat: 32g; Saturated Fat: 10g; Cholesterol: 140mg; Sodium: 180mg; Total Carbs: 24g; Dietary Fiber: 5g; Total Sugars: 8g; Protein: 57g

Sriracha Short Ribs

Servings: 4 | Prep Time: 5 Minutes | Cooking Time: 15 Minutes

Ingredients:

- 10 g sesame seeds
- 8 pork short ribs
- 118 g soy sauce
- 59 g rice wine vinegar
- 118 g chopped onion
- 2 garlic cloves, minced
- 15 g sesame oil
- 5 g sriracha
- 4 scallions, thinly sliced
- Salt and pepper to taste

Directions:

1. Put short ribs in a resealable bag along with soy sauce, vinegar, onion, garlic, sesame oil, Sriracha, half of the scallions, salt, and pepper. Seal the bag and toss to coat. Refrigerate for one hour.
2. Preheat air fryer to 190°C/380°F. Place the short ribs in the air fryer. Bake for 8-10 minutes, flipping once until crisp. When the ribs are done, garnish with remaining scallions and sesame seeds. Serve and enjoy!

Variations & Ingredients Tips:

- Use beef short ribs or country-style pork ribs for meatier bites
- Brush the ribs with honey or brown sugar in the last few minutes of cooking for a sticky glaze
- Serve with kimchi, pickled radish and steamed rice

Per Serving: Calories: 535; Total Fat: 43g; Saturated Fat: 14g; Cholesterol: 113mg; Sodium: 2319mg; Total Carbs: 9g; Dietary Fiber: 1g; Total Sugars: 3g; Protein: 27g

Tamari-seasoned Pork Strips

Servings: 4 | Prep Time: 10 Minutes | Cooking Time: 40 Minutes

Ingredients:

- 3 tablespoons olive oil
- 2 tablespoons tamari
- 2 teaspoons red chili paste
- 2 teaspoons yellow mustard
- 2 teaspoons granulated sugar
- 454 g pork shoulder strips
- 1 cup white rice, cooked
- 6 scallions, chopped
- ½ teaspoon garlic powder
- 1 tablespoon lemon juice
- 1 teaspoon lemon zest
- ½ teaspoon salt

Directions:

1. Add 2 tbsp of olive oil, tamari, chili paste, mustard, and sugar to a bowl and whisk until everything is well mixed. Set aside half of the marinade. Toss pork strips in the remaining marinade and put in the fridge for 30 minutes.
2. Preheat air fryer to 175°C/350°F. Place the pork strips in the frying basket and Air Fry for 16-18 minutes, tossing once. Transfer cooked pork to the bowl along with the remaining marinade and toss to coat. Set aside. In a medium bowl, stir in the cooked rice, garlic, lemon juice, lemon zest, and salt and cover. Spread on a serving plate. Arrange the pork strips over and top with scallions. Serve.

Variations & Ingredients Tips:

- Use chicken thighs or beef sirloin instead of pork
- Substitute tamari with soy sauce or coconut aminos
- Serve over cauliflower rice or zucchini noodles for low-carb

Per Serving: Calories: 466; Total Fat: 27g; Saturated Fat: 6g; Cholesterol: 100mg; Sodium: 998mg; Total Carbs: 28g; Dietary Fiber: 1g; Total Sugars: 3g; Protein: 31g

Seedy Rib Eye Steak Bites

Servings: 4 | Prep Time: 10 Minutes | Cooking Time: 20 Minutes

Ingredients:

- 454 g rib eye steak, cubed
- 2 garlic cloves, minced
- 2 tablespoons olive oil
- 1 tablespoon thyme, chopped
- 1 teaspoon ground fennel seeds
- Salt and pepper to taste
- 1 onion, thinly sliced

Directions:

1. Preheat air fryer to 190°C/380°F. Place the steak, garlic, olive oil, thyme, fennel seeds, salt, pepper, and onion in a bowl. Mix until all of the beef and onion are well coated. Put the seasoned steak mixture into the frying basket. Roast for 10 minutes, stirring once. Let sit for 5 minutes. Serve.

Variations & Ingredients Tips:

- Use sirloin, flank or skirt steak instead of ribeye
- Add some sliced bell peppers or mushrooms to the mix
- Serve over rice, pasta or salad greens for a complete meal

Per Serving: Calories: 318; Total Fat: 23g; Saturated Fat: 8g; Cholesterol: 81mg; Sodium: 100mg; Total Carbs: 3g; Dietary Fiber: 1g; Total Sugars: 1g; Protein: 24g

Kawaii Pork Roast

Servings: 6 | Prep Time: 10 Minutes | Cooking Time: 50 Minutes

Ingredients:

- Salt and white pepper to taste
- 2 tbsp soy sauce
- 2 tbsp honey

- 1 tbsp sesame oil
- 1/4 tsp ground ginger
- 1 tsp oregano
- 2 cloves garlic, minced
- 1 boneless pork loin (around 1.4kg)

Directions:

1. Preheat air fryer at 350°F/177°C. Mix all ingredients in a bowl. Massage mixture into all sides of pork loin. Place pork loin in the greased frying basket and Roast for 40 minutes, flipping once. Let rest onto a cutting board for 5 minutes before slicing into 25cm thick slices. Serve right away.

Variations & Ingredients Tips:

- Add grated ginger or Chinese five-spice powder for more flavor
- Brush the roast with additional honey glaze halfway through cooking
- Serve sliced pork over rice or sliced on sandwiches

Per Serving: Calories: 300; Total Fat: 14g; Saturated Fat: 4g; Cholesterol: 100mg; Sodium: 500mg; Total Carbs: 8g; Dietary Fiber: 0g; Total Sugars: 6g; Protein: 35g

Chorizo & Veggie Bake

Servings: 4 | Prep Time: 15 Minutes | Cooking Time: 40 Minutes

Ingredients:

- 1 cup halved Brussels sprouts
- 450 g baby potatoes, halved
- 1 cup baby carrots
- 1 onion, sliced
- 2 garlic cloves, sliced
- 2 tablespoons olive oil
- Salt and pepper to taste
- 450 g chorizo sausages, sliced
- 2 tablespoons Dijon mustard

Directions:

1. Preheat the air fryer to 190°C/370°F. Put the potatoes, Brussels sprouts, baby carrots, garlic, and onion in the frying basket and drizzle with olive oil. Sprinkle with salt and pepper; toss to coat.
2. Bake for 15 minutes or until the veggies are crisp but tender, shaking once during cooking.
3. Add the chorizo sausages to the fryer and cook for 8-12 minutes, shaking once until the sausages are hot and the veggies tender.
4. Drizzle with the mustard to serve.

Variations & Ingredients Tips:

- Use different types of sausage, such as Italian or bratwurst, for a variety of flavors.
- Add some bell peppers or zucchini to the vegetable mixture for extra color and nutrients.
- Serve the chorizo and veggie bake with a side of crusty bread or rice for a complete meal.

Per Serving: Calories: 610; Total Fat: 46g; Saturated Fat: 15g; Cholesterol: 85mg; Sodium: 1180mg; Total Carbs: 28g; Fiber: 5g; Sugars: 5g; Protein: 24g

Sirloin Steak Bites With Gravy

Servings: 4 | Prep Time: 10 Minutes | Cooking Time: 20 Minutes

Ingredients:

- 680 g sirloin steak, cubed
- 1 tablespoon olive oil
- 2 tablespoons cornstarch, divided
- 2 tablespoons soy sauce
- 2 tablespoons Worcestershire sauce
- 2 garlic cloves, minced
- Salt and pepper to taste
- ½ teaspoon smoked paprika
- ½ cup sliced red onion
- 2 fresh thyme sprigs
- ½ cup sliced mushrooms
- 1 cup beef broth
- 1 tablespoon butter

Directions:

1. Preheat air fryer to 200°C/400°F. Combine beef, olive oil, 1 tablespoon of cornstarch, garlic, pepper, Worcestershire sauce, soy sauce, thyme, salt, and paprika. Arrange the beef on the greased baking dish, then top with onions and mushrooms. Place the dish in the frying basket and bake for 4 minutes. While the beef is baking, whisk beef broth and the rest of the cornstarch in a small bowl. When the beef is ready, add butter and beef broth to the baking dish. Bake for another 5 minutes. Allow resting for 5 minutes. Serve and enjoy.

Variations & Ingredients Tips:

- Use chuck roast or stew meat instead of sirloin
- Add some baby potatoes or carrots to the dish
- Serve over mashed potatoes, egg noodles or rice

Per Serving: Calories: 382; Total Fat: 20g; Saturated Fat: 7g; Cholesterol: 122mg; Sodium: 809mg; Total Carbs: 8g; Dietary Fiber: 1g; Total Sugars: 2g; Protein: 41g

Honey Mustard Pork Roast

Servings: 4 | Prep Time: 10 Minutes | Cooking Time: 50 Minutes

Ingredients:

- 1 boneless pork loin roast
- 2 tbsp Dijon mustard
- 2 tsp olive oil
- 1 tsp honey
- 1 garlic clove, minced
- Salt and pepper to taste
- 1 tsp dried rosemary

Directions:

1. Preheat air fryer to 175°C/350°F. Whisk all ingredients in a bowl. Massage into loin on all sides. Place the loin in the

frying basket and Roast for 40 minutes, turning once. Let sit onto a cutting board for 5 minutes before slicing. Serve.

Variations & Ingredients Tips:

- Use whole grain or spicy brown mustard for a bolder flavor
- Add some smoked paprika or cumin to the rub for a smoky twist
- Slice and serve over a salad or in sandwiches for leftovers

Per Serving: Calories: 257; Total Fat: 11g; Saturated Fat: 3g; Cholesterol: 90mg; Sodium: 269mg; Total Carbs: 4g; Dietary Fiber: 0g; Total Sugars: 3g; Protein: 36g

Crispy Lamb Shoulder Chops

Servings: 3 | Prep Time: 10 Minutes | Cooking Time: 28 Minutes

Ingredients:

- ¾ cup all-purpose flour or gluten-free all-purpose flour
- 2 teaspoons mild paprika
- 2 teaspoons table salt
- 1½ teaspoons garlic powder
- 1½ teaspoons dried sage leaves
- 3 lamb shoulder chops (170 g each), any excess fat trimmed
- Olive oil spray

Directions:

1. Whisk the flour, paprika, salt, garlic powder, and sage in a large bowl until the mixture is of a uniform color. Add the chops and toss well to coat. Transfer them to a cutting board.
2. Preheat the air fryer to 190°C/375°F.
3. When the machine is at temperature, again dredge the chops one by one in the flour mixture. Lightly coat both sides of each chop with olive oil spray before putting it in the basket. Continue on with the remaining chop(s), leaving air space between them in the basket.
4. Air-fry, turning once, for 25 minutes, or until the chops are well browned and tender when pierced with the point of a paring knife. If the machine is at 180°C/360°F, you may need to add up to 3 minutes to the cooking time.
5. Use kitchen tongs to transfer the chops to a wire rack. Cool for 5 minutes before serving.

Variations & Ingredients Tips:

- Use different types of seasoning, such as herbs de Provence or Italian seasoning, for a variety of flavors.
- Add some grated Parmesan cheese or nutritional yeast to the flour mixture for a cheesy flavor.
- Serve the lamb chops with a side of roasted vegetables or mashed potatoes for a complete meal.

Per Serving: Calories: 520; Total Fat: 30g; Saturated Fat: 11g; Cholesterol: 150mg; Sodium: 1560mg; Total Carbs: 22g; Fiber: 1g; Sugars: 0g; Protein: 41g

Beef Brazilian Empanadas

Servings: 6 | Prep Time: 25 Minutes | Cooking Time: 40 Minutes

Ingredients:

- 1 cup shredded Pepper Jack cheese
- 80 g minced green bell pepper
- 1 cup shredded mozzarella
- 2 garlic cloves, chopped
- ⅓ onion, chopped
- 225 g ground beef
- 1 tsp allspice
- ½ tsp paprika
- ½ tsp chili powder
- Salt and pepper to taste
- 15 empanada wrappers
- 1 tbsp butter

Directions:

1. Spray a skillet with cooking oil. Over medium heat, stir-fry garlic, green pepper, and onion for 2 minutes or until aromatic. Add beef, allspice, chili, paprika, salt and pepper. Use a spoon to break up the beef. Cook until brown. Drain the excess fat. On a clean work surface, glaze each empanada wrapper edge with water using a basting brush to soften the crust. Mound 2-3 tbsp of meat onto each wrapper. Top with mozzarella and pepper Jack cheese. Fold one side of the wrapper to the opposite side. Press the edges with the back of a fork to seal. Preheat air fryer to 200°C/400°F. Place the empanadas in the air fryer and spray with cooking oil. Bake for 8 minutes, then flip the empanadas. Cook for another 4 minutes. Melt butter in a microwave-safe bowl for 20 seconds. Brush melted butter over the top of each empanada. Serve warm.

Variations & Ingredients Tips:

- Use ground chicken, turkey, or pork instead of beef for different fillings.
- Add diced potatoes, peas, or carrots to the filling for extra veggies.
- Serve with salsa, guacamole, or sour cream for dipping.

Per Serving: Calories: 495; Total Fat: 29g; Saturated Fat: 14g; Cholesterol: 81mg; Sodium: 621mg; Total Carbohydrates: 36g; Dietary Fiber: 2g; Total Sugars: 3g; Protein: 24g

Meat Loaves

Servings: 4 | Prep Time: 15 Minutes | Cooking Time: 19 Minutes

Ingredients:

- Sauce
- ¼ cup white vinegar
- ¼ cup brown sugar
- 2 tablespoons Worcestershire sauce
- ½ cup ketchup
- Meat Loaves
- 450 g very lean ground beef
- ⅔ cup dry bread (approx. 1 slice torn into small pieces)
- 1 egg
- ⅓ cup minced onion

- 1 teaspoon salt
- 2 tablespoons ketchup

Directions:

1. In a small saucepan, combine all sauce ingredients and bring to a boil. Remove from heat and stir to ensure that brown sugar dissolves completely.
2. In a large bowl, combine the beef, bread, egg, onion, salt, and ketchup. Mix well.
3. Divide meat mixture into 4 portions and shape each into a thick, round patty. Patties will be about 7.5 to 9 cm in diameter, and all four should fit easily into the air fryer basket at once.
4. Cook at 180°C/360°F for 18 minutes, until meat is well done. Baste tops of mini loaves with a small amount of sauce, and cook 1 minute.
5. Serve hot with additional sauce on the side.

Variations & Ingredients Tips:

- Use different types of ground meat, such as turkey or pork, for a variety of flavors.
- Add some grated carrot or zucchini to the meat mixture for extra moisture and nutrients.
- Serve the meat loaves with a side of mashed potatoes or green beans for a classic comfort food meal.

Per Serving: Calories: 330; Total Fat: 12g; Saturated Fat: 4.5g; Cholesterol: 115mg; Sodium: 1070mg; Total Carbs: 31g; Fiber: 1g; Sugars: 22g; Protein: 25g

Herby Lamb Chops

Servings: 2 | Prep Time: 10 Minutes | Cooking Time: 25 Minutes

Ingredients:

- 3 lamb chops
- 1 cup breadcrumbs
- 2 eggs, beaten
- Salt and pepper to taste
- ½ tbsp thyme
- ½ tbsp mint, chopped
- ½ tsp garlic powder
- ½ tsp ground rosemary
- ½ tsp cayenne powder
- ½ tsp ras el hanout

Directions:

1. Preheat air fryer to 160°C/320°F. Mix the breadcrumbs, thyme, mint, garlic, rosemary, cayenne, ras el hanout, salt, and pepper in a bowl. Dip the lamb chops in the beaten eggs, then coat with the crumb mixture. Air Fry for 14-16 minutes, turning once. Serve and enjoy!

Variations & Ingredients Tips:

- Use panko breadcrumbs for an extra crispy coating
- Add some lemon zest to the herb mixture for brightness
- Serve with mint yogurt sauce or chimichurri for dipping

Per Serving: Calories: 596; Total Fat: 35g; Saturated Fat: 14g; Cholesterol: 285mg; Sodium: 511mg; Total Carbs: 27g; Dietary Fiber: 2g; Total Sugars: 3g; Protein: 45g

Tuscan Chimichangas

Servings: 2 | Prep Time: 10 Minutes | Cooking Time: 8 Minutes

Ingredients:

- 113g Thinly sliced deli ham, chopped
- 1 cup Drained and rinsed canned white beans
- 1/2 cup (about 57g) Shredded semi-firm mozzarella
- 1/4 cup Chopped sun-dried tomatoes
- 1/4 cup Bottled Italian salad dressing, vinaigrette type
- 2 Burrito-size (30cm) flour tortilla(s)
- Olive oil spray

Directions:

1. Preheat the air fryer to 375°F/191°C.
2. Mix the ham, beans, cheese, tomatoes, and salad dressing in a bowl.
3. Lay a tortilla on a clean, dry work surface. Put all of the ham mixture in a narrow oval in the middle of the tortilla, if making one burrito; or half of this mixture, if making two. Fold the parts of the tortilla that are closest to the ends of the filling oval up and over the filling, then roll the tortilla tightly closed, but don't press down hard. Generously coat the tortilla with olive oil spray. Make a second filled tortilla, if necessary.
4. Set the filled tortilla(s) seam side down in the basket, with at least 1.25cm between them, if making two. Air-fry undisturbed for 8 minutes, or until crisp and lightly browned.
5. Use kitchen tongs and a nonstick-safe spatula to transfer the chimichanga(s) to a wire rack. Cool for 5 minutes before serving.

Variations & Ingredients Tips:

- Add sauteed spinach or kale to the filling
- Substitute feta or ricotta salata for the mozzarella
- Brush the tortillas with garlic olive oil before filling

Per Serving: Calories: 580; Total Fat: 25g; Saturated Fat: 8g; Cholesterol: 50mg; Sodium: 1370mg; Total Carbs: 60g; Dietary Fiber: 7g; Total Sugars: 7g; Protein: 28g

Balsamic Beef & Veggie Skewers

Servings: 4 | Prep Time: 15 Minutes | Cooking Time: 25 Minutes

Ingredients:

- 2 tbsp balsamic vinegar
- 2 tsp olive oil
- 1/2 tsp dried oregano
- Salt and pepper to taste
- 340g round steak, cubed
- 1 red bell pepper, sliced
- 1 yellow bell pepper, sliced
- 1 cup cherry tomatoes

Directions:

1. Preheat air fryer to 199°C/390°F.
2. In a bowl, mix balsamic vinegar, olive oil, oregano, salt and pepper.
3. Add steak cubes and toss to coat. Marinate for 10 minutes.
4. Thread steak, bell peppers and tomatoes onto 8 metal skewers, alternating ingredients.
5. Place skewers in air fryer basket in a single layer.
6. Air fry for 5-7 minutes, turning once, until steak is cooked through and veggies are tender.
7. Serve immediately.

Variations & Ingredients Tips:

- Use chicken or shrimp instead of beef.
- Add mushrooms, zucchini or onions to the skewers.
- Brush with reserved marinade halfway through cooking.

Per Serving: Calories: 170; Total Fat: 7g; Saturated Fat: 2g; Cholesterol: 50mg; Sodium: 65mg; Total Carbohydrates: 6g; Dietary Fiber: 1g; Total Sugars: 4g; Protein: 19g

Cowboy Rib Eye Steak

Servings: 2 | Prep Time: 5 Minutes | Cooking Time: 20 Minutes

Ingredients:

- ¼ cup barbecue sauce
- 1 clove garlic, minced
- ⅛ teaspoon chili pepper
- ¼ teaspoon sweet paprika
- ¼ teaspoon cumin
- 1 rib-eye steak

Directions:

1. Preheat air fryer to 200°C/400°F.
2. In a bowl, whisk the barbecue sauce, garlic, chili pepper, paprika, and cumin. Divide in half and brush the steak with half of the sauce.
3. Add steak to the lightly greased frying basket and Air Fry for 10 minutes until you reach your desired doneness, turning once and brushing with the remaining sauce.
4. Let rest for 5 minutes onto a cutting board before slicing.
5. Serve warm.

Variations & Ingredients Tips:

- Use different types of steak, such as sirloin or tenderloin, for a variety of flavors and textures.
- Add some smoked paprika or chipotle pepper to the sauce for a smoky and spicy flavor.
- Serve the steak with a side of roasted potatoes or grilled asparagus for a complete meal.

Per Serving: Calories: 280; Total Fat: 16g; Saturated Fat: 6g; Cholesterol: 75mg; Sodium: 460mg; Total Carbs: 9g; Fiber: 0g; Sugars: 7g; Protein: 24g

Pepperoni Bagel Pizzas

Servings: 4 | Prep Time: 10 Minutes | Cooking Time: 20 Minutes

Ingredients:

- 2 bagels, halved horizontally
- 2 cups shredded mozzarella
- ¼ cup grated Parmesan
- 1 cup passata
- 85 g sliced pepperoni
- 2 scallions, chopped
- 2 tablespoons minced fresh chives
- 1 teaspoon red chili flakes

Directions:

1. Preheat the air fryer to 190°C/375°F. Put the bagel halves, cut side up, in the frying basket.
2. Bake for 2-3 minutes until golden. Remove and top them with passata, pepperoni, scallions, and cheeses.
3. Put the bagels topping-side up to the frying basket and cook for 8-12 more minutes or until the bagels are hot and the cheese has melted and is bubbling.
4. Top with the chives and chili flakes and serve.

Variations & Ingredients Tips:

- Use different types of cheese, such as cheddar or provolone, for a variety of flavors.
- Add some sliced mushrooms or olives to the pizza for extra toppings.
- Serve the bagel pizzas with a side of marinara sauce or ranch dressing for dipping.

Per Serving: Calories: 390; Total Fat: 19g; Saturated Fat: 9g; Cholesterol: 50mg; Sodium: 990mg; Total Carbs: 32g; Fiber: 2g; Sugars: 5g; Protein: 24g

Easy-peasy Beef Sliders

Servings: 4 | Prep Time: 10 Minutes | Cooking Time: 25 Minutes

Ingredients:

- 454g ground beef
- 1/4 tsp cumin
- 1/4 tsp mustard powder
- 1/3 cup grated yellow onion
- 1/2 tsp smoked paprika
- Salt and pepper to taste

Directions:

1. Preheat air fryer to 175°C/350°F. Combine the ground beef, cumin, mustard, onion, paprika, salt, and black pepper in a bowl. Form mixture into 8 patties and make a slight indentation in the middle of each. Place beef patties in the greased frying basket and Air Fry for 8-10 minutes, flipping once. Serve right away and enjoy!

Variations & Ingredients Tips:

- Use ground turkey or chicken instead of beef
- Add shredded cheese like cheddar to the patty mixture
- Brush patties with BBQ sauce or garlic butter before serving

Per Serving: Calories: 265; Total Fat: 16g; Saturated Fat: 6g; Cholesterol: 75mg; Sodium: 185mg; Total Carbs: 2g; Dietary Fiber: 1g; Total Sugars: 1g; Protein: 26g

Kielbasa Chunks With Pineapple & Peppers

Servings: 2 | Prep Time: 5 Minutes | Cooking Time: 10 Minutes

Ingredients:

- 340g kielbasa sausage
- 240g bell pepper chunks (any color)
- 227g can pineapple chunks in juice, drained
- 1 tablespoon barbeque seasoning
- 1 tablespoon soy sauce
- Cooking spray

Directions:

1. Cut sausage into 25cm slices.
2. In a medium bowl, toss all ingredients together.
3. Spray air fryer basket with nonstick cooking spray.
4. Pour sausage mixture into the basket.
5. Cook at 390°F/199°C for approximately 5 minutes. Shake basket and cook an additional 5 minutes.

Variations & Ingredients Tips:

- Use turkey or chicken sausage for a leaner option
- Add thinly sliced onions or shallots to the mix
- Drizzle with teriyaki sauce instead of soy sauce

Per Serving: Calories: 505; Total Fat: 36g; Saturated Fat: 12g; Cholesterol: 105mg; Sodium: 2090mg; Total Carbs: 36g; Dietary Fiber: 3g; Total Sugars: 21g; Protein: 17g

Crispy Pork Pork Escalopes

Servings: 4 | Prep Time: 10 Minutes | Cooking Time: 20 Minutes

Ingredients:

- 4 pork loin steaks
- Salt and pepper to taste
- ¼ cup flour
- 2 tablespoons bread crumbs

Directions:

1. Preheat air fryer to 190°C/380°F.
2. Season pork with salt and pepper. In one shallow bowl, add flour. In another, add bread crumbs.
3. Dip the steaks first in the flour, then in the crumbs.
4. Place them in the fryer and spray with oil.
5. Bake for 12-14 minutes, flipping once until crisp.
6. Serve.

Variations & Ingredients Tips:

- Use different types of breading, such as panko or cornmeal, for a variety of textures.
- Add some grated Parmesan cheese or nutritional yeast to the breadcrumb mixture for a cheesy flavor.
- Serve the pork escalopes with a side of mashed potatoes or roasted vegetables for a complete meal.

Per Serving: Calories: 220; Total Fat: 8g; Saturated Fat: 2.5g; Cholesterol: 75mg; Sodium: 150mg; Total Carbs: 7g; Fiber: 0g; Sugars: 0g; Protein: 29g

Creamy Horseradish Roast Beef

Servings: 6 | Prep Time: 15 Minutes | Cooking Time: 65 Minutes + Chilling Time

Ingredients:

- 1 topside roast, tied
- Salt to taste
- 1 teaspoon butter, melted
- 2 tablespoons Dijon mustard
- 3 tablespoons prepared horseradish
- 1 garlic clove, minced
- ⅔ cup buttermilk
- 2 teaspoons red wine
- 1 tablespoon minced chives
- Salt and pepper to taste

Directions:

1. Preheat air fryer to 160°C/320°F.
2. Mix salt, butter, half of the mustard, 1 teaspoon of horseradish, and garlic until blended. Rub all over the roast.
3. Bake the roast in the air fryer for 30-35 minutes, flipping once until browned. Transfer to a cutting board and cover with foil. Let rest for 15 minutes.
4. In a bowl, mix buttermilk, horseradish, remaining mustard, chives, wine, salt, and pepper until smooth. Refrigerate.
5. When ready to serve, carve the roast into thin slices and serve with horseradish cream on the side.

Variations & Ingredients Tips:

- Use different types of mustard, such as whole grain or spicy brown, for a variety of flavors.
- Add some minced shallots or onion to the horseradish cream for extra flavor.
- Serve the roast beef with a side of roasted potatoes or green beans for a complete meal.

Per Serving: Calories: 320; Total Fat: 16g; Saturated Fat: 6g; Cholesterol: 105mg; Sodium: 520mg; Total Carbs: 5g; Fiber: 0g; Sugars: 3g; Protein: 38g

Barbecue Country-style Pork Ribs

Servings: 3 | Prep Time: 5 Minutes | Cooking Time: 30 Minutes

Ingredients:

- 3 225-g boneless country-style pork ribs
- 1½ teaspoons Mild smoked paprika
- 1½ teaspoons Light brown sugar
- ¾ teaspoon Onion powder
- ¾ teaspoon Ground black pepper
- ¼ teaspoon Table salt
- Vegetable oil spray

Directions:

1. Preheat the air fryer to 175°C/350°F. Set the ribs in a bowl on the counter as the machine heats.
2. Mix the smoked paprika, brown sugar, onion powder, pepper, and salt in a small bowl until well combined. Rub this mixture over all the surfaces of the country-style ribs. Generously coat the country-style ribs with vegetable oil spray.
3. Set the ribs in the basket with as much air space between them as possible. Air-fry undisturbed for 30 minutes, or until browned and sizzling and an instant-read meat thermometer inserted into one rib registers at least 65°C/145°F.
4. Use kitchen tongs to transfer the country-style ribs to a wire rack. Cool for 5 minutes before serving.

Variations & Ingredients Tips:

- For a spicier rub, add some cayenne pepper or chili powder.
- Brush the ribs with your favorite barbecue sauce during the last 5 minutes of cooking for extra flavor and stickiness.
- Serve with coleslaw, potato salad, or baked beans on the side.

Per Serving: Calories: 370; Total Fat: 26g; Saturated Fat: 8g; Cholesterol: 120mg; Sodium: 280mg; Total Carbohydrates: 4g; Dietary Fiber: 1g; Total Sugars: 3g; Protein: 31g

Indonesian Pork Satay

Servings: 4 | Prep Time: 20 Minutes | Cooking Time: 30 Minutes

Ingredients:

- 450g pork tenderloin, cubed
- 1/4 cup minced onion
- 2 garlic cloves, minced
- 1 jalapeño pepper, minced
- 2 tbsp lime juice
- 2 tbsp coconut milk
- 1/2 tbsp ground coriander
- 1/2 tsp ground cumin
- 2 tbsp peanut butter
- 2 tsp curry powder

Directions:

1. Combine the pork, onion, garlic, jalapeño, lime juice, coconut milk, peanut butter, ground coriander, cumin, and curry powder in a bowl. Stir well and allow to marinate for 10 minutes.
2. Preheat air fryer to 380°F/193°C. Use a holey spoon and take the pork out of the marinade and set the marinade aside. Poke 8 bamboo skewers through the meat, then place the skewers in the air fryer. Use a cooking brush to rub the marinade on each skewer, then Grill for 10-14 minutes, adding more marinade if necessary. The pork should be golden and cooked through when finished. Serve warm.

Variations & Ingredients Tips:

- Use chicken instead of pork for chicken satay
- Add some brown sugar or honey to the marinade for a sweet and savory flavor
- Serve with peanut dipping sauce and cucumber salad on the side

Per Serving: Calories: 325; Total Fat: 14g; Saturated Fat: 4g; Cholesterol: 95mg; Sodium: 220mg; Total Carbs: 11g; Dietary Fiber: 2g; Total Sugars: 3g; Protein: 36g

Crispy Ham And Eggs

Servings: 3 | Prep Time: 5 Minutes | Cooking Time: 9 Minutes

Ingredients:

- 2 cups rice-puff cereal, such as Rice Krispies
- ¼ cup maple syrup
- 225 g ¼- to 1.3-cm-thick ham steak (gluten-free, if a concern)
- 1 tablespoon unsalted butter
- 3 large eggs
- ⅛ teaspoon table salt
- ⅛ teaspoon ground black pepper

Directions:

1. Preheat the air fryer to 200°C/400°F.
2. Pour the cereal into a food processor, cover, and process until finely ground. Pour the ground cereal into a shallow soup plate or a small pie plate.
3. Smear the maple syrup on both sides of the ham, then set the ham into the ground cereal. Turn a few times, pressing gently, until evenly coated.
4. Set the ham steak in the basket and air-fry undisturbed for 5 minutes, or until browned.
5. Meanwhile, melt the butter in a medium or large nonstick skillet set over medium heat. Crack the eggs into the skillet and cook until the whites are set and the yolks are hot, about 3 minutes (or 4 minutes for a more set yolk). Season with the salt and pepper.
6. When the ham is ready, transfer it to a serving platter, then slip the eggs from the skillet on top of it. Divide into portions to serve.

Variations & Ingredients Tips:

- Use different types of cereal, such as cornflakes or breadcrumbs, for a variety of textures.
- Add some chopped fresh herbs, such as parsley or chives, to the eggs for extra flavor.
- Serve the ham and eggs with a side of roasted potatoes or sliced tomatoes for a classic breakfast.

Per Serving: Calories: 330; Total Fat: 16g; Saturated Fat: 6g; Cholesterol: 255mg; Sodium: 1070mg; Total Carbs: 27g; Fiber: 0g; Sugars: 16g; Protein: 20g

Pork Cutlets With Almond-lemon Crust

Servings: 3 | Prep Time: 15 Minutes | Cooking Time: 14 Minutes

Ingredients:

- ¾ cup Almond flour
- ¾ cup Plain dried bread crumbs (gluten-free, if a concern)
- 1½ teaspoons Finely grated lemon zest
- 1¼ teaspoons Table salt
- ¾ teaspoon Garlic powder
- ¾ teaspoon Dried oregano
- 1 Large egg white(s)
- 2 tablespoons Water
- 3 170 g center-cut boneless pork loin chops (about 2 cm thick)
- Olive oil spray

Directions:

1. Preheat the air fryer to 190°C/375°F.
2. Mix the almond flour, bread crumbs, lemon zest, salt, garlic powder, and dried oregano in a large bowl until well combined.
3. Whisk the egg white(s) and water in a shallow soup plate or small pie plate until uniform.
4. Dip a chop in the egg white mixture, turning it to coat all sides, even the ends. Let any excess egg white mixture slip back into the rest, then set it in the almond flour mixture. Turn it several times, pressing gently to coat it evenly. Generously coat the chop with olive oil spray, then set aside to dip and coat the remaining chop(s).
5. Set the chops in the basket with as much air space between them as possible. Air-fry undisturbed for 12 minutes, or until browned and crunchy. You may need to add 2 minutes to the cooking time if the machine is at 180°C/360°F.
6. Use kitchen tongs to transfer the chops to a wire rack. Cool for a few minutes before serving.

Variations & Ingredients Tips:

- Try using different nuts like pecans or hazelnuts in place of almonds
- Add some grated Parmesan cheese to the breading mixture for extra flavor
- Serve with a side of lemon wedges for squeezing over the cutlets

Per Serving: Calories: 499; Total Fat: 30g; Saturated Fat: 4g; Cholesterol: 116mg; Sodium: 1416mg; Total Carbs: 15g; Dietary Fiber: 4g; Total Sugars: 2g; Protein: 45g

Crispy Pork Medallions With Radicchio And Endive Salad

Servings: 4 | Prep Time: 20 Minutes | Cooking Time: 7 Minutes

Ingredients:

- 1 (225 g) pork tenderloin
- Salt and freshly ground black pepper
- ¼ cup flour
- 2 eggs, lightly beaten
- ¾ cup cracker meal
- 1 teaspoon paprika
- 1 teaspoon dry mustard
- 1 teaspoon garlic powder
- 1 teaspoon dried thyme
- 1 teaspoon salt
- Vegetable or canola oil, in spray bottle
- Vinaigrette
- ¼ cup white balsamic vinegar
- 2 tablespoons agave syrup (or honey or maple syrup)
- 1 tablespoon Dijon mustard
- Juice of ½ lemon
- 2 tablespoons chopped chervil or flat-leaf parsley
- Salt and freshly ground black pepper
- ½ cup extra-virgin olive oil
- Radicchio and Endive Salad
- 1 heart romaine lettuce, torn into large pieces
- ½ head radicchio, coarsely chopped
- 2 heads endive, sliced
- ½ cup cherry tomatoes, halved
- 85 g fresh mozzarella, diced
- Salt and freshly ground black pepper

Directions:

1. Slice the pork tenderloin into 2.5 cm slices. Using a meat pounder, pound the pork slices into thin 25 cm medallions. Generously season the pork with salt and freshly ground black pepper on both sides.
2. Set up a dredging station using three shallow dishes. Place the flour in one dish and the beaten eggs in a second dish. Combine the cracker meal, paprika, dry mustard, garlic powder, thyme and salt in a third dish.
3. Preheat the air fryer to 200°C/400°F.
4. Dredge the pork medallions in flour first and then into the beaten egg. Let the excess egg drip off and coat both sides of the medallions with the cracker meal crumb mixture. Spray both sides of the coated medallions with vegetable or canola oil.
5. Air-fry the medallions in two batches at 200°C/400°F for 5 minutes. Once you have air-fried all the medallions, flip them all over and return the first batch of medallions back into the air fryer on top of the second batch. Air-fry at 200°C/400°F for an additional 2 minutes.
6. While the medallions are cooking, make the salad and dressing. Whisk the white balsamic vinegar, agave syrup, Dijon mustard, lemon juice, chervil, salt and pepper together in a small bowl. Whisk in the olive oil slowly until

combined and thickened.
7. Combine the romaine lettuce, radicchio, endive, cherry tomatoes, and mozzarella cheese in a large salad bowl. Drizzle the dressing over the vegetables and toss to combine. Season with salt and freshly ground black pepper.
8. Serve the pork medallions warm on or beside the salad.

Variations & Ingredients Tips:

- Use different types of lettuce, such as arugula or spinach, for a variety of flavors and textures.
- Add some sliced red onion or shaved Parmesan cheese to the salad for extra flavor.
- Serve the pork medallions with a side of roasted potatoes or grilled asparagus for a complete meal.

Per Serving: Calories: 590; Total Fat: 41g; Saturated Fat: 9g; Cholesterol: 155mg; Sodium: 1340mg; Total Carbs: 22g; Fiber: 4g; Sugars: 8g; Protein: 35g

Baby Back Ribs

Servings: 4 | Prep Time: 10 Minutes | Cooking Time: 36 Minutes

Ingredients:

- 1 kg pork baby back rib rack(s)
- 1 tablespoon dried barbecue seasoning blend or rub (gluten-free, if a concern)
- 1 cup water
- 3 tablespoons purchased smooth barbecue sauce (gluten-free, if a concern)

Directions:

1. Preheat the air fryer to 180°C/350°F.
2. Cut the racks into 4- to 5-bone sections, about two sections for the small batch, three for the medium, and four for the large. Sprinkle both sides of these sections with the seasoning blend.
3. Pour the water into the bottom of the air-fryer drawer or into a tray placed under the rack. (The rack cannot then sit in water—adjust the amount of water for your machine.) Set the rib sections in the basket so that they're not touching. Air-fry for 30 minutes, turning once.
4. If using a tray with water, check it a couple of times to make sure it still has water in it or hasn't overflowed from the rendered fat.
5. Brush half the barbecue sauce on the exposed side of the ribs. Air-fry undisturbed for 3 minutes. Turn the racks over (but make sure they're still not touching), brush with the remaining sauce, and air-fry undisturbed for 3 minutes more, or until sizzling and brown.
6. Use kitchen tongs to transfer the racks to a cutting board. Let stand for 5 minutes, then slice between the bones to serve.

Variations & Ingredients Tips:

- Use different types of barbecue sauce, such as spicy or sweet, for a variety of flavors.
- Add some smoked paprika or chili powder to the seasoning blend for a smoky and spicy kick.
- Serve the baby back ribs with a side of corn on the cob or baked beans for a classic barbecue meal.

Per Serving: Calories: 580; Total Fat: 40g; Saturated Fat: 14g; Cholesterol: 175mg; Sodium: 650mg; Total Carbs: 7g; Fiber: 0g; Sugars: 5g; Protein: 48g

Oktoberfest Bratwursts

Servings: 4 | Prep Time: 5 Minutes | Cooking Time: 35 Minutes

Ingredients:

- ½ onion, cut into half-moons
- 450 g pork bratwurst links
- 2 cups beef broth
- 1 cup beer
- 2 cups drained sauerkraut
- 2 tablespoons German mustard

Directions:

1. Pierce each bratwurst with a fork twice. Place them along with beef broth, beer, 1 cup of water, and onion in a saucepan over high heat and bring to a boil. Lower the heat and simmer for 15 minutes. Drain.
2. Preheat air fryer to 200°C/400°F. Place bratwursts and onion in the frying basket and Air Fry for 3 minutes. Flip bratwursts, add the sauerkraut and cook for 3 more minutes.
3. Serve warm with mustard on the side.

Variations & Ingredients Tips:

- Use different types of beer, such as lager or ale, for a variety of flavors.
- Add some sliced bell peppers or carrots to the bratwurst mixture for extra vegetables.
- Serve the bratwursts in buns with a side of German potato salad or soft pretzels for an authentic Oktoberfest meal.

Per Serving: Calories: 450; Total Fat: 32g; Saturated Fat: 11g; Cholesterol: 80mg; Sodium: 1620mg; Total Carbs: 15g; Fiber: 3g; Sugars: 4g; Protein: 21g

Air-fried Roast Beef With Rosemary Roasted Potatoes

Servings: 8 | Prep Time: 15 Minutes | Cooking Time: 60 Minutes

Ingredients:

- 2.25 kg top sirloin roast
- Salt and freshly ground

- black pepper
- 1 teaspoon dried thyme
- 900 g red potatoes, halved or quartered
- 2 teaspoons olive oil
- 1 teaspoon very finely chopped fresh rosemary, plus more for garnish

Directions:

1. Start by making sure your roast will fit into the air fryer basket without touching the top element. Trim it if you have to in order to get it to fit nicely in your air fryer. (You can always save the trimmings for another use, like a beef sandwich.)
2. Preheat the air fryer to 180°C/360°F.
3. Season the beef all over with salt, pepper and thyme. Transfer the seasoned roast to the air fryer basket.
4. Air-fry at 180°C/360°F for 20 minutes. Turn the roast over and continue to air-fry at 180°C/360°F for another 20 minutes.
5. Toss the potatoes with the olive oil, salt, pepper and fresh rosemary. Turn the roast over again in the air fryer basket and toss the potatoes in around the sides of the roast. Air-fry the roast and potatoes at 180°C/360°F for another 20 minutes. Check the internal temperature of the roast with an instant-read thermometer, and continue to roast until the beef is 5° lower than your desired degree of doneness. (Rare - 55°C/130°F, Medium - 65°C/150°F, Well done - 75°C/170°F.) Let the roast rest for 5 to 10 minutes before slicing and serving. While the roast is resting, continue to air-fry the potatoes if desired for extra browning and crispiness.
6. Slice the roast and serve with the potatoes, adding a little more fresh rosemary if desired.

Variations & Ingredients Tips:

- Try using different cuts of beef, such as eye of round or tenderloin, for a variety of flavors and textures.
- Add some minced garlic or red pepper flakes to the potatoes for extra flavor.
- Serve the roast and potatoes with a side of horseradish sauce or gravy for a classic pairing.

Per Serving: Calories: 510; Total Fat: 25g; Saturated Fat: 9g; Cholesterol: 155mg; Sodium: 210mg; Total Carbs: 16g; Fiber: 2g; Sugars: 1g; Protein: 54g

Effortless Beef & Rice

Servings: 4 | Prep Time: 10 Minutes | Cooking Time: 35 Minutes

Ingredients:

- 227g ground beef
- 1 onion, chopped
- 1 celery stalk, chopped
- 3 garlic cloves, minced
- 2 cups cooked rice
- 1 tomato, chopped
- 3 tbsp tomato paste
- 2/3 cup beef broth
- 1 tsp smoked paprika
- 1/2 tsp dried oregano
- 1/2 tsp ground nutmeg
- Salt and pepper to taste

Directions:

1. Preheat air fryer to 188°C/370°F.
2. In a baking pan, combine ground beef, onion, celery and garlic. Break up beef with a fork.
3. Place pan in greased air fryer basket and cook for 5-7 minutes until beef is browned.
4. Add rice, tomato, tomato paste, broth, paprika, oregano, nutmeg, salt and pepper to the pan. Stir well.
5. Return pan to air fryer and cook for 10-13 minutes, stirring once, until heated through and ingredients are blended.
6. Serve hot.

Variations & Ingredients Tips:

- Use ground turkey or chicken instead of beef.
- Add frozen mixed vegetables to increase nutrients.
- Top with shredded cheese before serving.

Per Serving: Calories: 295; Total Fat: 12g; Saturated Fat: 4g; Cholesterol: 50mg; Sodium: 460mg; Total Carbs: 28g; Dietary Fiber: 3g; Total Sugars: 5g; Protein: 18g

Vegetarian Recipes

Green Bean & Baby Potato Mix

Servings: 4 | Prep Time: 10 Minutes | Cooking Time: 25 Minutes

Ingredients:

- 450g baby potatoes, halved
- 4 garlic cloves, minced
- 2 tbsp olive oil
- Salt and pepper to taste
- 1/2 tsp hot paprika
- 1/2 tbsp taco seasoning
- 1 tbsp chopped parsley
- 225g green beans, trimmed

Directions:

1. Preheat air fryer to 190°C/375°F.
2. Toss potatoes, garlic, olive oil, salt, pepper, hot paprika,

and taco seasoning in a bowl.
3. Arrange potatoes in the air fryer basket. Air Fry for 10 minutes, then stir in green beans.
4. Air Fry for 10 more minutes.
5. Serve hot sprinkled with parsley.

Variations & Ingredients Tips:

- Add diced onions or bell peppers for extra veggies.
- Sprinkle with grated parmesan before serving.
- Toss with fresh herbs like rosemary or thyme.

Per Serving: Calories: 160; Total Fat: 6g; Saturated Fat: 1g; Sodium: 200mg; Total Carbs: 24g; Dietary Fiber: 4g; Total Sugars: 3g; Protein: 4g

Honey Pear Chips

Servings: 4 | Prep Time: 10 Minutes | Cooking Time: 30 Minutes

Ingredients:

- 2 firm pears, thinly sliced
- 1 tbsp lemon juice
- ½ tsp ground cinnamon
- 1 tsp honey

Directions:

1. Preheat air fryer to 190°C/380°F.
2. Arrange the pear slices on the parchment-lined cooking basket. Drizzle with lemon juice and honey and sprinkle with cinnamon.
3. Air Fry for 6-8 minutes, shaking the basket once, until golden.
4. Leave to cool. Serve immediately or save for later in an airtight container. Good for 2 days.

Variations & Ingredients Tips:

- Substitute pears with apples or peaches for different flavors.
- Add a pinch of nutmeg or ginger for extra warmth and spice.
- Serve with a dollop of yogurt or ice cream for a sweet treat.

Per Serving: Calories: 70; Total Fat: 0g; Saturated Fat: 0g; Sodium: 0mg; Total Carbohydrates: 18g; Dietary Fiber: 3g; Total Sugars: 13g; Protein: 0g

Stuffed Portobellos

Servings: 4 | Prep Time: 20 Minutes | Cooking Time: 45 Minutes

Ingredients:

- 1 cup cherry tomatoes
- 2 ¼ tsp olive oil
- 3 tbsp grated mozzarella
- 1 cup chopped baby spinach
- 1 garlic clove, minced
- ¼ tsp dried oregano
- ¼ tsp dried thyme
- Salt and pepper to taste
- ¼ cup bread crumbs
- 4 portobello mushrooms, stemmed and gills removed
- 1 tbsp chopped parsley

Directions:

1. Preheat air fryer to 180°C/360°F.
2. Combine tomatoes, ¼ teaspoon olive oil, and salt in a small bowl. Arrange in a single layer in the parchment-lined air fryer basket and Air Fry for 10 minutes. Stir and flatten the tomatoes with the back of a spoon, then Air Fry for another 6-8 minutes.
3. Transfer the tomatoes to a medium bowl and combine with spinach, garlic, oregano, thyme, pepper, bread crumbs, and the rest of the olive oil.
4. Place the mushrooms on a work surface with the gills facing up. Spoon tomato mixture and mozzarella cheese equally into the mushroom caps and transfer the mushrooms to the air fryer basket.
5. Air Fry for 8-10 minutes until the mushrooms have softened and the tops are golden.
6. Garnish with chopped parsley and serve.

Variations & Ingredients Tips:

- Substitute portobello mushrooms with large button mushrooms or zucchini boats.
- Add cooked quinoa, rice, or ground meat to the filling for a heartier dish.
- Top with a drizzle of balsamic glaze or pesto sauce before serving.

Per Serving: Calories: 130; Total Fat: 7g; Saturated Fat: 2g; Sodium: 200mg; Total Carbohydrates: 12g; Dietary Fiber: 3g; Total Sugars: 4g; Protein: 7g

Caprese-style Sandwiches

Servings: 2 | Prep Time: 10 Minutes | Cooking Time: 20 Minutes

Ingredients:

- 2 tbsp balsamic vinegar
- 4 sandwich bread slices
- 60 grams mozzarella shreds
- 3 tbsp pesto sauce
- 2 tomatoes, sliced
- 8 basil leaves
- 8 baby spinach leaves
- 2 tbsp olive oil

Directions:

1. Preheat air fryer at 175°C/350°F. Drizzle balsamic vinegar on the bottom of bread slices and smear with pesto sauce. Then, layer mozzarella cheese, tomatoes, baby spinach leaves and basil leaves on top. Add top bread slices. Rub the outside top and bottom of each sandwich with olive oil. Place them in the frying basket and Bake for 5 minutes,

flipping once. Serve right away.

Variations & Ingredients Tips:

- Use ciabatta, focaccia, or sourdough bread for a rustic sandwich.
- Add sliced prosciutto or salami for a non-vegetarian version.
- Drizzle with extra balsamic glaze or olive oil before serving for added flavor.

Per Serving (1 sandwich): Calories: 450; Cholesterol: 25mg; Total Fat: 28g; Saturated Fat: 7g; Sodium: 670mg; Total Carbohydrates: 37g; Dietary Fiber: 4g; Total Sugars: 8g; Protein: 16g

Veggie Burgers

Servings: 4 | Prep Time: 10 Minutes | Cooking Time: 15 Minutes

Ingredients:

- 2 cans black beans, rinsed and drained
- 1/2 cup cooked quinoa
- 1/2 cup shredded raw sweet potato
- 1/4 cup diced red onion
- 2 teaspoons ground cumin
- 1 teaspoon coriander powder
- 1/2 teaspoon salt
- Oil for misting or cooking spray
- 8 slices bread
- Suggested toppings: lettuce, tomato, red onion, Pepper Jack cheese, guacamole

Directions:

1. In a medium bowl, mash the beans with a fork.
2. Add the quinoa, sweet potato, onion, cumin, coriander, and salt and mix well with the fork.
3. Shape into 4 patties, each 2-cm thick.
4. Mist both sides with oil or cooking spray and also mist the basket.
5. Cook at 200°C/390°F for 15 minutes.
6. Follow the recipe for Toast, Plain & Simple.
7. Pop the veggie burgers back in the air fryer for a minute or two to reheat if necessary.
8. Serve on the toast with your favorite burger toppings.

Variations & Ingredients Tips:

- Use different beans like kidney or pinto.
- Add breadcrumbs or oats for binding if needed.
- Bake instead of air fry for a firmer patty.

Per Serving: Calories: 262; Total Fat: 3g; Saturated Fat: 0g; Sodium: 604mg; Total Carbohydrates: 48g; Dietary Fiber: 15g; Total Sugars: 4g; Protein: 14g

Meatless Kimchi Bowls

Servings: 4 | Prep Time: 10 Minutes | Cooking Time: 20 Minutes

Ingredients:

- 2 cups canned chickpeas
- 1 carrot, julienned
- 6 scallions, sliced
- 1 zucchini, diced
- 2 tbsp coconut aminos
- 2 tsp sesame oil
- 1 tsp rice vinegar
- 2 tsp granulated sugar
- 1 tbsp gochujang
- ¼ tsp salt
- ½ cup kimchi
- 2 tsp roasted sesame seeds

Directions:

1. Preheat air fryer to 180°C/350°F.
2. Combine all ingredients, except for the kimchi, 2 scallions, and sesame seeds, in a baking pan.
3. Place the pan in the air fryer basket and Air Fry for 6 minutes.
4. Toss in kimchi and cook for 2 more minutes.
5. Divide between 2 bowls and garnish with the remaining scallions and sesame seeds.
6. Serve immediately.

Variations & Ingredients Tips:

- Use tempeh or tofu instead of chickpeas for a different protein source.
- Add sliced mushrooms or eggplant for meatier texture.
- Adjust gochujang amount to make it spicier or milder.

Per Serving: Calories: 210; Total Fat: 6g; Saturated Fat: 1g; Sodium: 690mg; Total Carbohydrates: 31g; Dietary Fiber: 8g; Total Sugars: 8g; Protein: 10g

Curried Potato, Cauliflower And Pea Turnovers

Servings: 4 | Prep Time: 30 Minutes | Cooking Time: 40 Minutes

Ingredients:

- Dough:
- 2 cups all-purpose flour
- ½ teaspoon baking powder
- 1 teaspoon salt
- freshly ground black pepper
- ¼ teaspoon dried thyme
- 60 ml canola oil
- 120 to 160 ml water
- Turnover Filling:
- 1 tablespoon canola or vegetable oil
- 1 onion, finely chopped
- 1 clove garlic, minced
- 1 tablespoon grated fresh ginger
- ½ teaspoon cumin seeds
- ½ teaspoon fennel seeds
- 1 teaspoon curry powder
- 2 russet potatoes, diced
- 240 grams cauliflower florets
- ½ cup frozen peas
- 2 tablespoons chopped fresh cilantro
- salt and freshly ground black pepper
- 2 tablespoons butter, melted
- mango chutney, for serving

Directions:

1. Start by making the dough. Combine the flour, baking powder, salt, pepper and dried thyme in a mixing bowl or the bowl of a stand mixer. Drizzle in the canola oil and pinch it together with your fingers to turn the flour into a crumby mixture. Stir in the water (enough to bring the dough together). Knead the dough for 5 minutes or so until it is smooth. Add a little more water or flour as needed. Let the dough rest while you make the turnover filling.
2. Preheat a large skillet on the stovetop over medium-high heat. Add the oil and sauté the onion until it starts to become tender – about 4 minutes. Add the garlic and ginger and continue to cook for another minute. Add the dried spices and toss everything to coat. Add the potatoes and cauliflower to the skillet and pour in 360 ml of water. Simmer everything together for 20 to 25 minutes, or until the potatoes are soft and most of the water has evaporated. If the water has evaporated and the vegetables still need more time, just add a little water and continue to simmer until everything is tender. Stir well, crushing the potatoes and cauliflower a little as you do so. Stir in the peas and cilantro, season to taste with salt and freshly ground black pepper and set aside to cool.
3. Divide the dough into 4 balls. Roll the dough balls out into 6-mm thick circles. Divide the cooled potato filling between the dough circles, placing a mound of the filling on one side of each piece of dough, leaving an empty border around the edge of the dough. Brush the edges of the dough with a little water and fold one edge of circle over the filling to meet the other edge of the circle, creating a half moon. Pinch the edges together with your fingers and then press the edge with the tines of a fork to decorate and seal.
4. Preheat the air fryer to 190°C/380°F.
5. Spray or brush the air fryer basket with oil. Brush the turnovers with the melted butter and place 2 turnovers into the air fryer basket. Air-fry for 15 minutes. Flip the turnovers over and air-fry for another 5 minutes. Repeat with the remaining 2 turnovers.
6. These will be very hot when they come out of the air fryer. Let them cool for at least 20 minutes before serving warm with mango chutney.

Variations & Ingredients Tips:

- Use sweet potatoes instead of russet potatoes for a sweeter filling.
- Add diced bell peppers, carrots, or spinach to the veggie mixture for extra nutrition.
- Serve with yogurt raita or mint chutney for dipping.

Per Serving (1 turnover): Calories: 520; Cholesterol: 15mg; Total Fat: 24g; Saturated Fat: 7g; Sodium: 670mg; Total Carbohydrates: 68g; Dietary Fiber: 6g; Total Sugars: 6g; Protein: 11g

Tandoori Paneer Naan Pizza

Servings: 4 | Prep Time: 15 Minutes | Cooking Time: 10 Minutes

Ingredients:

- 6 tablespoons plain Greek yogurt, divided
- 1 1/4 teaspoons garam masala, divided
- 1/2 teaspoon turmeric, divided
- 1/4 teaspoon garlic powder
- 1/2 teaspoon paprika, divided
- 1/2 teaspoon black pepper, divided
- 85g paneer, cut into small cubes
- 1 tablespoon extra-virgin olive oil
- 2 teaspoons minced garlic
- 4 cups baby spinach
- 2 tablespoons marinara sauce
- 1/4 teaspoon salt
- 2 plain naan breads (approximately 15cm in diameter)
- 1/2 cup shredded part-skim mozzarella cheese

Directions:

1. Preheat air fryer to 180°C/350°F.
2. Marinate paneer in 2 tbsp yogurt, 1/2 tsp garam masala, 1/4 tsp turmeric, garlic powder, 1/4 tsp paprika, 1/4 tsp pepper for 1 hour.
3. Sauté garlic in olive oil, then add spinach and remaining yogurt, marinara, spices and salt.
4. Divide spinach mixture between naans, top with marinated paneer.
5. Air fry one naan at a time for 4 mins. Top with 1/4 cup mozzarella and cook 4 more mins.
6. Repeat with second naan. Serve warm.

Variations & Ingredients Tips:

- Use naan alternatives like pita or tortilla for the base.
- Add sautéed onions, bell peppers or mushrooms to the topping.
- Brush naans with garlic butter before baking.

Per Serving: Calories: 252; Total Fat: 11g; Saturated Fat: 4g; Sodium: 592mg; Total Carbohydrates: 28g; Dietary Fiber: 3g; Total Sugars: 5g; Protein: 12g

Tomato & Squash Stuffed Mushrooms

Servings: 2 | Prep Time: 10 Minutes | Cooking Time: 15 Minutes

Ingredients:

- 12 whole white button mushrooms
- 3 tsp olive oil
- 2 tbsp diced zucchini
- 1 tsp soy sauce
- 1/4 tsp salt
- 2 tbsp tomato paste
- 1 tbsp chopped parsley

Directions:

1. Preheat air fryer to 180°C/350°F.
2. Remove the stems from the mushrooms. Chop the stems finely and set in a bowl. Brush 1 tsp of olive oil around the top ridge of mushroom caps.
3. To the bowl of the stem, add all ingredients, except for parsley, and mix.
4. Divide and press mixture into tops of mushroom caps.
5. Place the mushrooms in the air fryer basket and Air Fry for 5 minutes.
6. Top with parsley. Serve.

Variations & Ingredients Tips:

- Use portobello mushrooms instead of button mushrooms for a larger appetizer.
- Substitute zucchini with eggplant, yellow squash, or bell peppers.
- Add grated Parmesan cheese or bread crumbs to the filling for extra flavor and texture.

Per Serving: Calories: 130; Total Fat: 10g; Saturated Fat: 1.5g; Sodium: 490mg; Total Carbohydrates: 7g; Dietary Fiber: 2g; Total Sugars: 4g; Protein: 4g

Thai Peanut Veggie Burgers

Servings: 6 | Prep Time: 20 Minutes | Cooking Time: 14 Minutes

Ingredients:

- One 440-gram can cannellini beans
- 1 teaspoon minced garlic
- ¼ cup chopped onion
- 1 Thai chili pepper, sliced
- 2 tablespoons natural peanut butter
- ½ teaspoon black pepper
- ½ teaspoon salt
- ⅓ cup all-purpose flour (optional)
- ½ cup cooked quinoa
- 1 large carrot, grated
- 1 cup shredded red cabbage
- ¼ cup peanut dressing
- ¼ cup chopped cilantro
- 6 Hawaiian rolls
- 6 butterleaf lettuce leaves

Directions:

1. Preheat the air fryer to 180°C/350°F.
2. To a blender or food processor fitted with a metal blade, add the beans, garlic, onion, chili pepper, peanut butter, pepper, and salt. Pulse for 5 to 10 seconds. Do not over process. The mixture should be coarse, not smooth.
3. Remove from the blender or food processor and spoon into a large bowl. Mix in the cooked quinoa and carrots. At this point, the mixture should begin to hold together to form small patties. If the dough appears to be too sticky (meaning you likely processed a little too long), add the flour to hold the patties together.
4. Using a large spoon, form 8 equal patties out of the batter.
5. Liberally spray a metal trivet with olive oil spray and set in the air fryer basket. Place the patties into the basket, leaving enough space to be able to turn them with a spatula.
6. Cook for 7 minutes, flip, and cook another 7 minutes.
7. Remove from the heat and repeat with additional patties.
8. To serve, place the red cabbage in a bowl and toss with peanut dressing and cilantro. Place the veggie burger on a bun, and top with a slice of lettuce and cabbage slaw.

Variations & Ingredients Tips:

- Use chickpeas or black beans instead of cannellini beans.
- Substitute peanut butter with almond butter or sunflower seed butter.
- Add shredded beetroot or zucchini to the patty mixture.

Per Serving: Calories: 340; Total Fat: 11g; Saturated Fat: 2g; Sodium: 580mg; Total Carbohydrates: 50g; Dietary Fiber: 9g; Total Sugars: 8g; Protein: 13g

Spicy Vegetable And Tofu Shake Fry

Servings: 4 | Prep Time: 20 Minutes | Cooking Time: 17 Minutes

Ingredients:

- 4 teaspoons canola oil, divided
- 2 tablespoons rice wine vinegar
- 1 tablespoon sriracha chili sauce
- ¼ cup soy sauce*
- ½ teaspoon toasted sesame oil
- 1 teaspoon minced garlic
- 1 tablespoon minced fresh ginger
- 227 grams extra firm tofu
- ½ cup vegetable stock or water
- 1 tablespoon honey
- 1 tablespoon cornstarch
- ½ red onion, chopped
- 1 red or yellow bell pepper, chopped
- 1 cup green beans, cut into 5-cm lengths
- 113 grams mushrooms, sliced
- 2 scallions, sliced
- 2 tablespoons fresh cilantro leaves
- 2 teaspoons toasted sesame seeds

Directions:

1. Combine 1 tablespoon of the oil, vinegar, sriracha sauce, soy sauce, sesame oil, garlic and ginger in a small bowl. Cut the tofu into bite-sized cubes and toss the tofu in with the marinade while you prepare the other vegetables. When you are ready to start cooking, remove the tofu from the marinade and set it aside. Add the water, honey and cornstarch to the marinade and bring to a simmer on the stovetop, just until the sauce thickens. Set the sauce aside.
2. Preheat the air fryer to 200°C/400°F.
3. Toss the onion, pepper, green beans and mushrooms in a bowl with a little canola oil and season with salt. Air-fry at 200°C/400°F for 11 minutes, shaking the basket and tossing the vegetables every few minutes. When the vegetables are cooked to your preferred doneness, remove them from

the air fryer and set aside.
4. Add the tofu to the air fryer basket and air-fry at 200°C/400°F for 6 minutes, shaking the basket a few times during the cooking process. Add the vegetables back to the basket and air-fry for another minute.
5. Transfer the vegetables and tofu to a large bowl, add the scallions and cilantro leaves and toss with the sauce. Serve over rice with sesame seeds sprinkled on top.

Variations & Ingredients Tips:

- Swap tofu for tempeh or seitan for a different plant-based protein.
- Use any mix of vegetables like broccoli, cauliflower, carrots, or snow peas.
- Adjust the amount of sriracha for more or less heat.

Per Serving: Calories: 260; Total Fat: 15g; Saturated Fat: 1.5g; Sodium: 950mg; Total Carbohydrates: 23g; Dietary Fiber: 4g; Total Sugars: 11g; Protein: 13g

Golden Fried Tofu

Servings: 4 | Prep Time: 10 Minutes | Cooking Time: 20 Minutes

Ingredients:

- 1/4 cup flour
- 1/4 cup cornstarch
- 1 tsp garlic powder
- 1/4 tsp onion powder
- Salt and pepper to taste
- 400g firm tofu, cubed
- 2 tbsp chopped cilantro

Directions:

1. Preheat air fryer to 200°C/390°F.
2. Combine flour, cornstarch, garlic powder, onion powder, salt and pepper in a bowl.
3. Place tofu cubes in the flour mixture and toss to coat.
4. Spray tofu with oil and place in a single layer in the greased frying basket.
5. Air Fry for 14-16 minutes, flipping once, until golden and crunchy.
6. Top with chopped cilantro and serve immediately.

Variations & Ingredients Tips:

- Use panko breadcrumbs instead of flour for extra crunch.
- Toss cooked tofu in buffalo or teriyaki sauce.
- Serve over salad or stir-fried veggies.

Per Serving: Calories: 170; Total Fat: 5g; Saturated Fat: 0.5g; Sodium: 20mg; Total Carbs: 21g; Dietary Fiber: 2g; Total Sugars: 1g; Protein: 11g

Gorgeous Jalapeño Poppers

Servings: 6 | Prep Time: 15 Minutes | Cooking Time: 25 Minutes

Ingredients:

- 6 center-cut bacon slices, halved
- 6 jalapeños, halved lengthwise
- 115g cream cheese
- 1/4 cup grated Gruyere cheese
- 2 tbsp chopped chives

Directions:

1. Scoop out seeds and membranes of the jalapeño halves, discard.
2. Combine cream cheese, Gruyere cheese, and chives in a bowl.
3. Fill the jalapeño halves with the cream cheese filling using a small spoon.
4. Wrap each pepper with a slice of bacon and secure with a toothpick.
5. Preheat air fryer to 165°C/325°F.
6. Put the stuffed peppers in a single layer on the greased frying basket and Bake until the peppers are tender, cheese is melted, and the bacon is browned, 11-13 minutes.
7. Serve warm.

Variations & Ingredients Tips:

- Use turkey bacon for a lighter option.
- Mix shredded cheddar into the cream cheese filling.
- Add a drizzle of ranch dressing when serving.

Per Serving: Calories: 180; Total Fat: 14g; Saturated Fat: 7g; Sodium: 330mg; Total Carbs: 4g; Dietary Fiber: 1g; Total Sugars: 2g; Protein: 9g

Bengali Samosa With Mango Chutney

Servings: 4 | Prep Time: 20 Minutes | Cooking Time: 65 Minutes

Ingredients:

- ¼ tsp ground fenugreek seeds
- 1 cup diced mango
- 1 tbsp minced red onion
- 2 tsp honey
- 1 tsp minced ginger
- 1 tsp apple cider vinegar
- 1 phyllo dough sheet
- 2 tbsp olive oil
- 1 potato, mashed
- ½ tsp garam masala
- ¼ tsp ground turmeric
- ⅛ tsp chili powder
- ¼ tsp ground cumin
- ½ cup green peas
- 2 scallions, chopped

Directions:

1. Mash mango in a small bowl until chunky. Stir in onion, ginger, honey, and vinegar. Save in the fridge until ready to use. Place the mashed potato in a bowl. Add half of the olive oil, garam masala, turmeric, chili powder, ground fenugreek seeds, cumin, and salt and stir until mostly smooth. Stir in peas and scallions.
2. Preheat air fryer to 220°C/425°F. Lightly flour a flat work surface and transfer the phyllo dough. Cut into 8 equal portions and roll each portion to 6-mm thick rounds. Divide

the potato filling between the dough rounds. Fold in three sides and pinch at the meeting point, almost like a pyramid. Arrange the samosas in the frying basket and brush with the remaining olive oil. Bake for 10 minutes, then flip the samosas. Bake for another 4-6 minutes until the crust is crisp and golden. Serve with mango chutney.

Variations & Ingredients Tips:

- Use store-bought mango chutney for a quicker version.
- Substitute phyllo dough with puff pastry or wonton wrappers if desired.
- Add chopped cashews or raisins to the potato filling for extra texture and flavor.

Per Serving: Calories: 310; Cholesterol: 0mg; Total Fat: 13g; Saturated Fat: 2g; Sodium: 180mg; Total Carbohydrates: 45g; Dietary Fiber: 5g; Total Sugars: 15g; Protein: 6g

Asparagus, Mushroom And Cheese Soufflés

Servings: 3 | Prep Time: 20 Minutes | Cooking Time: 21 Minutes

Ingredients:

- butter
- grated Parmesan cheese
- 3 button mushrooms, thinly sliced
- 8 spears asparagus, sliced 1.25-cm long
- 1 teaspoon olive oil
- 1 tablespoon butter
- 4½ teaspoons flour
- pinch paprika
- pinch ground nutmeg
- salt and freshly ground black pepper
- ½ cup milk
- ½ cup grated Gruyère cheese or other Swiss cheese
- 2 eggs, separated

Directions:

1. Butter three 170-g ramekins and dust with grated Parmesan cheese. (Butter the ramekins and then coat the butter with Parmesan by shaking it around in the ramekin and dumping out any excess.)
2. Preheat the air fryer to 200°C/400°F.
3. Toss the mushrooms and asparagus in a bowl with the olive oil. Transfer the vegetables to the air fryer and air-fry for 7 minutes, shaking the basket once or twice to redistribute the ingredients while they cook.
4. While the vegetables are cooking, make the soufflé base. Melt the butter in a saucepan on the stovetop over medium heat. Add the flour, stir and cook for a minute or two. Add the paprika, nutmeg, salt and pepper. Whisk in the milk and bring the mixture to a simmer to thicken. Remove the pan from the heat and add the cheese, stirring to melt. Let the mixture cool for just a few minutes and then whisk the egg yolks in, one at a time. Stir in the cooked mushrooms and asparagus. Let this soufflé base cool.
5. In a separate bowl, whisk the egg whites to soft peak stage (the point at which the whites can almost stand up on the end of your whisk). Fold the whipped egg whites into the soufflé base, adding a little at a time.
6. Preheat the air fryer to 165°C/330°F.
7. Transfer the batter carefully to the buttered ramekins, leaving about 1.25-cm at the top. Place the ramekins into the air fryer basket and air-fry for 14 minutes. The soufflés should have risen nicely and be brown on top. Serve immediately.

Variations & Ingredients Tips:

- Use different vegetables like spinach, broccoli, or bell peppers for a variety of flavors.
- Substitute Gruyère with cheddar, gouda, or brie for a different cheese profile.
- Serve the soufflés with a side salad or crusty bread for a complete meal.

Per Serving (1 soufflé): Calories: 290; Cholesterol: 165mg; Total Fat: 20g; Saturated Fat: 11g; Sodium: 410mg; Total Carbohydrates: 12g; Dietary Fiber: 1g; Total Sugars: 4g; Protein: 16g

Vietnamese Gingered Tofu

Servings: 4 | Prep Time: 10 Minutes | Cooking Time: 25 Minutes

Ingredients:

- 1 package extra-firm tofu, cubed
- 4 tsp shoyu (soy sauce)
- 1 tsp onion powder
- 1/2 tsp garlic powder
- 1/2 tsp ginger powder
- 1/2 tsp turmeric powder
- Black pepper to taste
- 2 tbsp nutritional yeast
- 1 tsp dried rosemary
- 1 tsp dried dill
- 2 tsp cornstarch
- 2 tsp sunflower oil

Directions:

1. Sprinkle the tofu with shoyu and toss to coat.
2. Add the onion, garlic, ginger, turmeric, and pepper. Gently toss to coat.
3. Add the yeast, rosemary, dill, and cornstarch. Toss to coat.
4. Dribble with the oil and toss again.
5. Preheat air fryer to 200°C/390°F. Spray the basket with oil.
6. Put the tofu in the basket and Bake for 7 minutes.
7. Remove, shake gently, and cook for another 7 minutes or until crispy and golden.
8. Serve warm.

Variations & Ingredients Tips:

- Use tamari or coconut aminos instead of soy sauce.
- Add chili garlic sauce or sriracha for a spicy kick.
- Toss with chopped scallions before serving.

Per Serving: Calories: 132; Total Fat: 7g; Saturated Fat: 1g;

Sodium: 514mg; Total Carbohydrates: 8g; Dietary Fiber: 2g; Total Sugars: 1g; Protein: 13g

Powerful Jackfruit Fritters

Servings: 4 | Prep Time: 20 Minutes | Cooking Time: 30 Minutes

Ingredients:

- 1 can jackfruit, chopped
- 1 egg, beaten
- 1 tbsp Dijon mustard
- 1 tbsp mayonnaise
- 1 tbsp prepared horseradish
- 2 tbsp grated yellow onion
- 2 tbsp chopped parsley
- 2 tbsp chopped nori
- 2 tbsp flour
- 1 tbsp Cajun seasoning
- ¼ tsp garlic powder
- ¼ tsp salt
- 2 lemon wedges

Directions:

1. In a bowl, combine jackfruit, egg, mustard, mayonnaise, horseradish, onion, parsley, nori, flour, Cajun seasoning, garlic, and salt. Let chill in the fridge for 15 minutes.
2. Preheat air fryer to 180°C/350°F.
3. Divide the mixture into 12 balls. Place them in the air fryer basket and Air Fry for 10 minutes.
4. Serve with lemon wedges.

Variations & Ingredients Tips:

- Substitute jackfruit with canned artichoke hearts or hearts of palm.
- Use Old Bay seasoning instead of Cajun for a different spice profile.
- Serve with tartar sauce or spicy remoulade.

Per Serving: Calories: 120; Total Fat: 5g; Saturated Fat: 1g; Sodium: 730mg; Total Carbohydrates: 16g; Dietary Fiber: 3g; Total Sugars: 6g; Protein: 4g

Spaghetti Squash And Kale Fritters With Pomodoro Sauce

Servings: 3 | Prep Time: 20 Minutes | Cooking Time: 45 Minutes

Ingredients:

- 680g spaghetti squash (about half a large or a whole small squash)
- Olive oil
- 1/2 onion, diced
- 1/2 red bell pepper, diced
- 2 cloves garlic, minced
- 4 cups coarsely chopped kale
- Salt and freshly ground black pepper
- 1 egg
- 1/3 cup breadcrumbs, divided*
- 1/3 cup grated Parmesan cheese
- 1/2 teaspoon dried rubbed sage
- Pinch nutmeg
- 2 tablespoons olive oil
- 1/2 onion, chopped
- 1 to 2 cloves garlic, minced
- 1 (800g) can peeled tomatoes
- 1/4 cup red wine
- 1 teaspoon Italian seasoning
- 2 tablespoons chopped fresh basil, plus more for garnish
- Salt and freshly ground black pepper
- 1/2 teaspoon sugar (optional)

Directions:

1. Preheat the air fryer to 190°C/370°F.
2. Cut the spaghetti squash in half lengthwise and remove the seeds. Rub with olive oil and season with salt and pepper. Air fry for 30 minutes, flipping halfway.
3. Sauté onions, pepper, garlic and kale. Transfer to a bowl and let cool.
4. Make Pomodoro sauce: Sauté onion and garlic. Add tomatoes, wine, seasoning and basil. Simmer 20 mins. Season.
5. Scrape spaghetti squash flesh onto a sheet pan and let cool.
6. Add squash to kale mix with egg, breadcrumbs, cheese, spices and seasoning. Form 6 portions and brush with oil.
7. Air fry fritters at 190°C/370°F for 15 minutes, flipping halfway.
8. Serve fritters warm with Pomodoro sauce and garnish with basil.

Variations & Ingredients Tips:

- Substitute panko for regular breadcrumbs.
- Use plant-based parmesan for a vegan version.
- Add sun-dried tomatoes or olives to the fritter batter.

Per Serving: Calories: 389; Total Fat: 18g; Saturated Fat: 4g; Sodium: 585mg; Total Carbohydrates: 45g; Dietary Fiber: 7g; Total Sugars: 12g; Protein: 14g

Basil Green Beans

Servings: 4 | Prep Time: 5 Minutes | Cooking Time: 15 Minutes

Ingredients:

- 680 grams green beans, trimmed
- 1 tbsp olive oil
- 1 tbsp fresh basil, chopped
- Garlic salt to taste

Directions:

1. Preheat air fryer to 200°C/400°F. Coat the green beans with olive oil in a large bowl. Combine with fresh basil and garlic salt. Put the beans in the frying basket and Air Fry for 7-9 minutes, shaking once until the beans begin to brown. Serve warm and enjoy!

Variations & Ingredients Tips:

- Add sliced almonds or chopped bacon for extra crunch and flavor.

- Substitute basil with other fresh herbs like parsley, thyme, or oregano.
- Drizzle with balsamic vinegar or lemon juice before serving for a tangy twist.

Per Serving: Calories: 70; Cholesterol: 0mg; Total Fat: 4g; Saturated Fat: 0.5g; Sodium: 75mg; Total Carbohydrates: 9g; Dietary Fiber: 4g; Total Sugars: 4g; Protein: 2g

Sushi-style Deviled Eggs

Servings: 4 | Prep Time: 15 Minutes | Cooking Time: 20 Minutes

Ingredients:

- ¼ cup crabmeat, shells discarded
- 4 eggs
- 2 tbsp mayonnaise
- ½ tsp soy sauce
- ¼ avocado, diced
- ¼ tsp wasabi powder
- 2 tbsp diced cucumber
- 1 sheet nori, sliced
- 8 jarred pickled ginger slices
- 1 tsp toasted sesame seeds
- 2 spring onions, sliced

Directions:

1. Preheat air fryer to 130°C/260°F.
2. Place the eggs in muffin cups to avoid bumping around and cracking during the cooking process. Add silicone cups to the air fryer basket and Air Fry for 15 minutes.
3. Remove and plunge the eggs immediately into an ice bath to cool, about 5 minutes. Carefully peel and slice them in half lengthwise.
4. Spoon yolks into a separate medium bowl and arrange white halves on a large plate. Mash the yolks with a fork. Stir in mayonnaise, soy sauce, avocado, and wasabi powder until smooth. Mix in cucumber and spoon into white halves.
5. Scatter eggs with crabmeat, nori, pickled ginger, spring onions and sesame seeds to serve.

Variations & Ingredients Tips:

- Use smoked salmon or cooked shrimp instead of crabmeat.
- Add a drizzle of sriracha or hot sauce for extra heat.
- Garnish with furikake seasoning or bonito flakes.

Per Serving: Calories: 160; Total Fat: 12g; Saturated Fat: 3g; Sodium: 310mg; Total Carbohydrates: 4g; Dietary Fiber: 2g; Total Sugars: 1g; Protein: 10g

Vegetable Side Dishes Recipes

Mushrooms

Servings: 4 | Prep Time: 10 Minutes | Cooking Time: 12 Minutes

Ingredients:

- 227g whole white button mushrooms
- 1/2 teaspoon salt
- 1/8 teaspoon pepper
- 1/4 teaspoon garlic powder
- 1/4 teaspoon onion powder
- 5 tablespoons potato starch
- 1 egg, beaten
- 3/4 cup panko breadcrumbs
- Oil for misting or cooking spray

Directions:

1. Place mushrooms in a bowl. Add salt, pepper, garlic and onion powders and stir to coat.
2. Add potato starch and toss mushrooms until well coated.
3. Dip mushrooms in beaten egg, then roll in panko crumbs. Mist with oil spray.
4. Place mushrooms in air fryer basket. Stack them if needed.
5. Cook at 199°C/390°F for 5 minutes. Shake basket, then cook 7 more minutes until crispy.

Variations & Ingredients Tips:

- Use breadcrumbs instead of panko for a different texture.
- Add parmesan or ranch seasoning to the breading.
- Serve with ranch, blue cheese or marinara for dipping.

Per Serving: Calories: 138; Total Fat: 2g; Saturated Fat: 1g; Cholesterol: 47mg; Sodium: 524mg; Total Carbohydrates: 26g; Dietary Fiber: 2g; Total Sugars: 1g; Protein: 5g

Fried Pearl Onions With Balsamic Vinegar And Basil

Servings: 2 | Prep Time: 5 Minutes | Cooking Time: 10 Minutes

Ingredients:

- 454g fresh pearl onions
- 1 tablespoon olive oil
- Salt and freshly ground black pepper
- 1 teaspoon high quality aged balsamic vinegar
- 1 tablespoon chopped fresh basil leaves (or mint)

Directions:

1. Preheat air fryer to 200°C/400°F.
2. Decide to peel onions before or after cooking. Trim root ends if peeling first.
3. Toss pearl onions with olive oil, salt and pepper.
4. Air fry for 10 minutes, shaking basket a couple times during cooking. Add 2-3 mins for larger onions.
5. Let onions cool slightly and slip off any remaining skins.
6. Toss onions with balsamic vinegar and basil.
7. Serve.

Variations & Ingredients Tips:

- Use shallots instead of pearl onions.
- Add a pinch of red pepper flakes for heat.
- Substitute fresh thyme or parsley for the basil.

Per Serving: Calories: 135; Total Fat: 6g; Saturated Fat: 1g; Cholesterol: 0mg; Sodium: 10mg; Total Carbs: 18g; Fiber: 3g; Sugars: 6g; Protein: 2g

Layered Mixed Vegetables

Servings: 4 | Prep Time: 15 Minutes | Cooking Time: 30 Minutes

Ingredients:

- 1 Yukon gold potato, sliced
- 1 eggplant, sliced
- 1 carrot, thinly sliced
- 1/4 cup minced onions
- 3 garlic cloves, minced
- 3/4 cup milk
- 2 tbsp cornstarch
- 1/2 tsp dried thyme

Directions:

1. Preheat air fryer to 190°C/380°F.
2. In layers, add the potato, eggplant, carrot, onion, and garlic to a baking pan.
3. Combine the milk, cornstarch, and thyme in a bowl, then pour this mix over the veggies.
4. Put the pan in the air fryer and bake for 15 minutes. The casserole should be golden on top with softened veggies.
5. Serve immediately.

Variations & Ingredients Tips:

- Add sliced zucchini or summer squash to the layers.
- Use almond or oat milk instead of regular milk.
- Top with breadcrumbs or grated cheese before baking.

Per Serving: Calories: 117; Total Fat: 1g; Saturated Fat: 0.4g; Cholesterol: 2mg; Sodium: 56mg; Total Carbs: 24g; Dietary Fiber: 5g; Total Sugars: 6g; Protein: 4g

Asparagus Wrapped In Pancetta

Servings: 4 | Prep Time: 10 Minutes | Cooking Time: 30 Minutes

Ingredients:

- 20 asparagus trimmed
- Salt and pepper pepper
- 4 pancetta slices
- 1 tbsp fresh sage, chopped

Directions:

1. Sprinkle the asparagus with fresh sage, salt and pepper. Toss to coat.
2. Make 4 bundles of 5 spears by wrapping the center of the bunch with one slice of pancetta.
3. Preheat air fryer to 204°C/400°F.
4. Put the bundles in the greased frying basket and Air Fry for 8-10 minutes or until the pancetta is brown and the asparagus are starting to char on the edges.
5. Serve immediately.

Variations & Ingredients Tips:

- Wrap in prosciutto instead of pancetta.
- Brush with balsamic glaze before serving.
- Add a sprinkle of parmesan before wrapping.

Per Serving: Calories: 100; Total Fat: 5g; Saturated Fat: 2g; Cholesterol: 15mg; Sodium: 230mg; Total Carbs: 3g; Fiber: 1g; Sugars: 1g; Protein: 10g

Zucchini Boats With Ham And Cheese

Servings: 4 | Prep Time: 10 Minutes | Cooking Time: 12 Minutes

Ingredients:

- 2 15-cm-long zucchini
- 60 g thinly sliced deli ham, any rind removed, meat roughly chopped
- 4 dry-packed sun-dried tomatoes, chopped
- 80 ml purchased pesto
- 60 g packaged mini croutons
- 30 g shredded semi-firm mozzarella cheese

Directions:

1. Preheat the air fryer to 190°C/375°F. Split the zucchini in half lengthwise and use a flatware spoon or a serrated grapefruit spoon to scoop out the insides of the halves, leaving at least a 6-mm border all around the zucchini half. (You can save the scooped out insides to add to soups and stews—or even freeze it for a much later use.) Mix the ham, sun-dried tomatoes, pesto, croutons, and half the

cheese in a bowl until well combined. Pack this mixture into the zucchini "shells." Top them with the remaining cheese. Set them stuffing side up in the basket without touching (even a fraction of an cm between them is enough room). Air-fry undisturbed for 12 minutes, or until softened and browned, with the cheese melted on top. Use a non-stick-safe spatula to transfer the zucchini boats stuffing side up on a wire rack. Cool for 5 or 10 minutes before serving.

Variations & Ingredients Tips:

- Use prosciutto, salami, or bacon instead of ham for a different flavor.
- Add chopped olives, artichoke hearts, or roasted red peppers to the filling for a Mediterranean twist.
- Sprinkle with red pepper flakes, Italian seasoning, or fresh herbs before serving for extra flavor.

Per Serving: Calories: 202; Total Fat: 15g; Saturated Fat: 4g; Cholesterol: 23mg; Sodium: 531mg; Total Carbohydrates: 10g; Dietary Fiber: 2g; Total Sugars: 4g; Protein: 8g

Patatas Bravas

Servings: 4 | Prep Time: 10 Minutes | Cooking Time: 35 Minutes

Ingredients:

- 454g baby potatoes
- 1 onion, chopped
- 4 garlic cloves, minced
- 2 jalapeño peppers, minced
- 2 tsp olive oil
- 2 tsp ground chile de árbol
- 1/2 tsp ground cumin
- 1/2 tsp dried oregano

Directions:

1. Preheat air fryer to 190°C/370°F.
2. Put the potatoes, onion, garlic, jalapeños in a bowl and stir.
3. Pour in olive oil and stir again to coat.
4. Season with ground chile de árbol, cumin, and oregano.
5. Put the bowl in the air fryer basket and air fry for 22-28 minutes, shaking once.
6. Serve hot.

Variations & Ingredients Tips:

- Use a blend of chili powders like ancho and chipotle.
- Add chopped chorizo or bacon.
- Drizzle with garlic aioli or sour cream before serving.

Per Serving: Calories: 112; Total Fat: 3g; Saturated Fat: 0g; Cholesterol: 0mg; Sodium: 36mg; Total Carbohydrates: 20g; Dietary Fiber: 3g; Total Sugars: 2g; Protein: 3g

Onions

Servings: 4 | Prep Time: 5 Minutes | Cooking Time: 18 Minutes

Ingredients:

- 2 yellow onions (Vidalia or 1015 recommended)
- Salt and pepper
- 1/4 teaspoon ground thyme
- 1/4 teaspoon smoked paprika
- 2 teaspoons olive oil
- 28g Gruyère cheese, grated

Directions:

1. Peel onions and halve lengthwise (vertically).
2. Sprinkle cut sides of onions with salt, pepper, thyme, and paprika.
3. Place each onion half, cut-surface up, on a large square of aluminum foil. Pull sides of foil up to cup around onion. Drizzle cut surface of onions with oil.
4. Crimp foil at top to seal closed.
5. Place wrapped onions in air fryer basket and cook at 199°C/390°F for 18 minutes. When done, onions should be soft enough to pierce with fork but still slightly firm.
6. Open foil just enough to sprinkle each onion with grated cheese.
7. Cook for 30 seconds to 1 minute to melt cheese.

Variations & Ingredients Tips:

- Use sweet or red onions instead of yellow.
- Mix grated cheese with breadcrumbs before topping for a crispy crust.
- Add a pat of butter to the center before wrapping for extra richness.

Per Serving: Calories: 93; Total Fat: 5g; Saturated Fat: 2g; Cholesterol: 5mg; Sodium: 86mg; Total Carbohydrates: 11g; Dietary Fiber: 2g; Total Sugars: 5g; Protein: 3g

Greek-inspired Ratatouille

Servings: 6 | Prep Time: 15 Minutes | Cooking Time: 40 Minutes

Ingredients:

- 1 cup cherry tomatoes
- 1/2 bulb fennel, finely sliced
- 2 russet potatoes, cubed
- 1/2 cup tomatoes, cubed
- 1 eggplant, cubed
- 1 zucchini, cubed
- 1 red onion, chopped
- 1 red bell pepper, chopped
- 2 garlic cloves, minced
- 1 tsp dried mint
- 1 tsp dried parsley
- 1 tsp dried oregano
- Salt and pepper to taste
- 1/4 tsp red pepper flakes
- 1/3 cup olive oil
- 1 can tomato paste
- 1/4 cup vegetable broth

Directions:

1. Preheat air fryer to 160°C/320°F.
2. Mix the potatoes, tomatoes, fennel, eggplant, zucchini, onion, bell pepper, garlic, mint, parsley, oregano, salt, black pepper, and red pepper flakes in a bowl.

3. Whisk the olive oil, tomato paste, broth, and 1/4 cup of water in a small bowl. Toss the mixture with the vegetables.
4. Pour the coated vegetables into the air frying basket in a single layer and roast for 20 minutes.
5. Stir well and spread out again. Roast for an additional 10 minutes, then repeat the process and cook for another 10 minutes.
6. Serve and enjoy!

Variations & Ingredients Tips:

- Add chickpeas or white beans for extra protein.
- Swap zucchini for yellow squash.
- Use fresh herbs instead of dried.

Per Serving: Calories: 210; Total Fat: 14g; Saturated Fat: 2g; Cholesterol: 0mg; Sodium: 120mg; Total Carbohydrates: 21g; Dietary Fiber: 5g; Total Sugars: 8g; Protein: 3g

Sweet Potato Fries

Servings: 3 | Prep Time: 10 Minutes | Cooking Time: 20 Minutes

Ingredients:

- 2 sweet potatoes (280 g each)
- Vegetable oil spray
- To taste coarse sea salt or kosher salt

Directions:

1. Preheat the air fryer to 200°C/400°F.
2. Peel the sweet potato(es), then cut lengthwise into 6 mm thick slices. Cut these slices lengthwise into 6 mm thick matchsticks. Place these matchsticks in a bowl and coat them with vegetable oil spray. Toss well, spray them again, and toss several times to make sure they're all evenly coated.
3. When the machine is at temperature, pour the sweet potato matchsticks into the basket, spreading them out in as close to an even layer as possible. Air-fry for 20 minutes, tossing and rearranging the matchsticks every 5 minutes, until lightly browned and crisp.
4. Pour the contents of the basket into a bowl, add some salt to taste, and toss well to coat.

Variations & Ingredients Tips:

- Use different types of seasoning, such as cinnamon sugar or chili powder, for a unique flavor.
- Add some grated Parmesan cheese or nutritional yeast for a cheesy flavor.
- Serve the fries with a dipping sauce, such as ranch dressing or chipotle mayo.

Per Serving: Calories: 140; Total Fat: 0g; Saturated Fat: 0g; Cholesterol: 0mg; Sodium: 180mg; Total Carbs: 33g; Fiber: 5g; Sugars: 8g; Protein: 2g

Almond Green Beans

Servings: 4 | Prep Time: 5 Minutes | Cooking Time: 20 Minutes

Ingredients:

- 2 cups green beans, trimmed
- 1/4 cup slivered almonds
- 2 tbsp butter, melted
- Salt and pepper to taste
- 2 tsp lemon juice
- Lemon zest and slices

Directions:

1. Preheat air fryer at 190°C/375°F. Add almonds to the frying basket and Air Fry for 2 minutes, tossing once. Set aside in a small bowl.
2. Combine the remaining ingredients, except 1 tbsp of butter, in a bowl.
3. Place green beans in the frying basket and Air Fry for 10 minutes, tossing once. Then, transfer them to a large serving dish.
4. Scatter with the melted butter, lemon juice and roasted almonds and toss. Serve immediately garnished with lemon zest and lemon slices.

Variations & Ingredients Tips:

- Use hazelnut or pecan pieces instead of almonds.
- Toss with garlic butter instead of plain butter.
- Add crushed red pepper flakes for a kick of heat.

Per Serving: Calories: 148; Total Fat: 11g; Saturated Fat: 3g; Cholesterol: 12mg; Sodium: 53mg; Total Carbs: 9g; Fiber: 4g; Sugars: 4g; Protein: 4g

Lovely Mac'n'cheese

Servings: 4 | Prep Time: 10 Minutes | Cooking Time: 40 Minutes

Ingredients:

- 2 cups grated American cheese
- 4 cups elbow macaroni
- 3 eggs, beaten
- 1/2 cup sour cream
- 4 tbsp butter
- 1/2 tsp mustard powder
- 1/2 tsp salt
- 1 cup milk

Directions:

1. Preheat air fryer to 180°C/350°F.
2. Bring a pot of salted water to a boil and cook the macaroni following package instructions. Drain.
3. Add 1 1/2 cups cheese and butter to the hot macaroni and stir to melt.
4. Mix the eggs, milk, sour cream, mustard powder, and salt in a bowl and add to the macaroni; mix gently.
5. Spoon mixture into a greased baking dish and transfer to

air fryer.
6. Bake for 15 minutes. Sprinkle with remaining 1/2 cup cheese.
7. Cook 5-8 more minutes until top is bubbling and golden.
8. Serve.

Variations & Ingredients Tips:

- Add cooked bacon, ham or peas to the macaroni mixture.
- Use a blend of cheeses like cheddar and parmesan.
- Top with breadcrumb topping before baking.

Per Serving: Calories: 634; Total Fat: 37g; Saturated Fat: 21g; Cholesterol: 199mg; Sodium: 835mg; Total Carbs: 52g; Dietary Fiber: 2g; Total Sugars: 5g; Protein: 24g

Corn On The Cob

Servings: 4 | Prep Time: 5 Minutes | Cooking Time: 12 Minutes

Ingredients:

- 2 large ears fresh corn
- Olive oil for misting
- Salt (optional)

Directions:

1. Shuck corn, remove silks, and wash.
2. Cut or break each ear in half crosswise.
3. Spray corn with olive oil.
4. Cook at 198°C/390°F for 12 minutes or until browned as much as you like.
5. Serve plain or with coarsely ground salt.

Variations & Ingredients Tips:

- Brush with garlic butter or herb butter before cooking.
- Sprinkle with chili lime seasoning after cooking.
- Add grated parmesan or cotija cheese.

Per Serving: Calories: 120; Total Fat: 3g; Saturated Fat: 0g; Cholesterol: 0mg; Sodium: 10mg; Total Carbs: 22g; Fiber: 3g; Sugars: 5g; Protein: 4g

Southern Okra Chips

Servings: 2 | Prep Time: 10 Minutes | Cooking Time: 20 Minutes

Ingredients:

- 2 eggs
- 60 ml whole milk
- 60 ml bread crumbs
- 60 ml cornmeal
- 1 tablespoon Cajun seasoning
- Salt and pepper to taste
- ⅛ teaspoon chili pepper
- 225 g okra, sliced
- 1 tablespoon butter, melted

Directions:

1. Preheat air fryer at 200°C/400°F.
2. Beat the eggs and milk in a bowl.
3. In another bowl, combine the remaining ingredients, except okra and butter.
4. Dip okra chips in the egg mixture, then dredge them in the breadcrumbs mixture.
5. Place okra chips in the greased frying basket and Roast for 7 minutes, shake once and brush with melted butter.
6. Serve right away.

Variations & Ingredients Tips:

- Use panko breadcrumbs or crushed crackers instead of regular breadcrumbs for a crunchier texture.
- Add some grated Parmesan cheese or nutritional yeast to the breadcrumb mixture for a cheesy flavor.
- Serve the okra chips with a dipping sauce, such as ranch dressing or remoulade sauce.

Per Serving: Calories: 320; Total Fat: 16g; Saturated Fat: 6g; Cholesterol: 205mg; Sodium: 840mg; Total Carbs: 33g; Fiber: 4g; Sugars: 5g; Protein: 13g

Blistered Green Beans

Servings: 3 | Prep Time: 5 Minutes | Cooking Time: 10 Minutes

Ingredients:

- 340g Green beans, trimmed on both ends
- 1½ tablespoons Olive oil
- 3 tablespoons Pine nuts
- 1½ tablespoons Balsamic vinegar
- 1½ teaspoons Minced garlic
- ¾ teaspoon Table salt
- ¾ teaspoon Ground black pepper

Directions:

1. Preheat the air fryer to 200°C/400°F.
2. Toss the green beans and oil in a large bowl until all the green beans are glistening.
3. When the machine is at temperature, pile the green beans into the basket. Air-fry for 10 minutes, tossing often to rearrange the green beans in the basket, or until blistered and tender.
4. Dump the contents of the basket into a serving bowl. Add the pine nuts, vinegar, garlic, salt, and pepper. Toss well to coat and combine. Serve warm or at room temperature.

Variations & Ingredients Tips:

- Add crushed red pepper flakes for a kick of heat.
- Substitute walnuts or sliced almonds for the pine nuts.
- Toss with grated parmesan before serving.

Per Serving: Calories: 150; Total Fat: 11g; Saturated Fat: 1g;

Cholesterol: 0mg; Sodium: 460mg; Total Carbs: 10g; Fiber: 4g; Sugars: 4g; Protein: 4g

Veggie Fritters

Servings: 4 | Prep Time: 15 Minutes | Cooking Time: 35 Minutes

Ingredients:

- ¼ cup crumbled feta cheese
- 1 grated zucchini
- ¼ cup Parmesan cheese
- 2 tbsp minced onion
- 1 tbsp garlic powder
- 1 tbsp flour
- 1 tbsp cornmeal
- 1 tbsp butter, melted
- 1 egg
- 2 tsp chopped dill
- 2 tsp chopped parsley
- Salt and pepper to taste
- 1 cup bread crumbs

Directions:

1. Preheat air fryer at 175°C/350°F. Squeeze grated zucchini between paper towels to remove excess moisture. In a bowl, combine all ingredients except breadcrumbs. Form mixture into 12 balls, about 2 tbsp each. In a shallow bowl, add breadcrumbs. Roll each ball in breadcrumbs, covering all sides. Place fritters on an ungreased pizza pan. Place in the frying basket and air fry for 11 minutes, flipping once. Serve.

Variations & Ingredients Tips:

- Add grated carrots, sweet potatoes, or beets for a colorful twist.
- Use goat cheese, ricotta, or mozzarella instead of feta for a different flavor profile.
- Serve with tzatziki sauce, marinara sauce, or ranch dressing for dipping.

Per Serving: Calories: 264; Total Fat: 14g; Saturated Fat: 7g; Cholesterol: 74mg; Sodium: 566mg; Total Carbohydrates: 25g; Dietary Fiber: 2g; Total Sugars: 3g; Protein: 11g

Simple Peppared Carrot Chips

Servings: 4 | Prep Time: 5 Minutes | Cooking Time: 15 Minutes

Ingredients:

- 3 carrots, cut into coins
- 1 tablespoon sesame oil
- Salt and pepper to taste

Directions:

1. Preheat air fryer at 190°C/375°F.
2. Combine all ingredients in a bowl.
3. Place carrots in the frying basket and Roast for 10 minutes, tossing once.
4. Serve right away.

Variations & Ingredients Tips:

- Try using different types of seasoning, such as garlic powder, cumin, or smoked paprika for a unique flavor.
- For a sweeter version, toss the carrots with a little honey or maple syrup before cooking.
- Serve the carrot chips with a dipping sauce, such as hummus or ranch dressing.

Per Serving: Calories: 60; Total Fat: 4g; Saturated Fat: 0.5g; Cholesterol: 0mg; Sodium: 135mg; Total Carbs: 6g; Fiber: 2g; Sugars: 3g; Protein: 1g

Mediterranean Roasted Vegetables

Servings: 4 | Prep Time: 10 Minutes | Cooking Time: 30 Minutes

Ingredients:

- 1 red bell pepper, cut into chunks
- 1 cup sliced mushrooms
- 1 cup green beans, diced
- 1 zucchini, sliced
- 1/3 cup diced red onion
- 3 garlic cloves, sliced
- 2 tbsp olive oil
- 1 tsp rosemary
- 1/2 tsp flaked sea salt

Directions:

1. Preheat air fryer to 180°C/350°F.
2. Add the bell pepper, mushrooms, green beans, red onion, zucchini, rosemary, and garlic to a bowl and mix.
3. Spritz with olive oil and stir until well-coated.
4. Put the veggies in the frying basket and air fry for 14-18 minutes until crispy and softened.
5. Serve sprinkled with flaked sea salt.

Variations & Ingredients Tips:

- Add diced eggplant or cherry tomatoes.
- Use balsamic vinegar instead of olive oil.
- Toss with fresh basil or parmesan after cooking.

Per Serving: Calories: 88; Total Fat: 5g; Saturated Fat: 1g; Cholesterol: 0mg; Sodium: 106mg; Total Carbohydrates: 10g; Dietary Fiber: 3g; Total Sugars: 5g; Protein: 3g

Cheesy Texas Toast

Servings: 2 | Prep Time: 5 Minutes | Cooking Time: 4 Minutes

Ingredients:

- 2 2.5cm-thick slices Italian bread (each about 10cm across)
- 4 teaspoons Softened butter
- 2 teaspoons Minced garlic
- ¼ cup (about 21g) Finely grated Parmesan cheese

Directions:

1. Preheat the air fryer to 200°C/400°F.
2. Spread one side of each bread slice with 2 tsp butter. Sprinkle with 1 tsp minced garlic, followed by 2 tbsp grated cheese.
3. When the machine is at temperature, put the bread slices cheese side up in the basket with space between them.
4. Air-fry undisturbed for 4 minutes, or until browned and crunchy.
5. Use a nonstick-safe spatula to transfer the toasts cheese side up to a wire rack. Cool for 5 minutes before serving.

Variations & Ingredients Tips:

- Add dried Italian seasoning or crushed red pepper to the butter.
- Use different cheese varieties like cheddar, provolone or asiago.
- Brush with garlic butter instead of plain butter.

Per Serving: Calories: 320; Total Fat: 18g; Saturated Fat: 9g; Cholesterol: 35mg; Sodium: 820mg; Total Carbs: 30g; Fiber: 1g; Sugars: 1g; Protein: 10g

Hawaiian Brown Rice

Servings: 4 | Prep Time: 10 Minutes | Cooking Time: 12 Minutes

Ingredients:

- 113g ground sausage
- 1 teaspoon butter
- 1/4 cup minced onion
- 1/4 cup minced bell pepper
- 2 cups cooked brown rice
- 227g can crushed pineapple, drained

Directions:

1. Shape sausage into 3 or 4 thin patties. Cook at 200°C/390°F for 6 to 8 minutes or until well done. Remove from air fryer, drain, and crumble. Set aside.
2. Place butter, onion, and bell pepper in baking pan. Cook at 200°C/390°F for 1 minute and stir. Cook 4 minutes longer or just until vegetables are tender.
3. Add sausage, rice, and pineapple to vegetables and stir together.
4. Cook at 200°C/390°F for 2 minutes, until heated through.

Variations & Ingredients Tips:

- Use chicken or pork instead of sausage.
- Add diced ham or spam for a Hawaiian twist.
- Stir in raisins, cashews or green onions.

Per Serving: Calories: 280; Total Fat: 10g; Saturated Fat: 3g; Cholesterol: 30mg; Sodium: 360mg; Total Carbs: 38g; Dietary Fiber: 3g; Total Sugars: 8g; Protein: 10g

Honey-mustard Asparagus Puffs

Servings: 4 | Prep Time: 10 Minutes | Cooking Time: 35 Minutes

Ingredients:

- 8 asparagus spears
- 1/2 sheet puff pastry
- 2 tbsp honey mustard
- 1 egg, lightly beaten

Directions:

1. Preheat the air fryer to 190°C/375°F.
2. Spread the pastry with honey mustard and cut it into 8 strips.
3. Wrap the pastry, honey mustard-side in, around the asparagus.
4. Put a rack in the frying basket and lay the asparagus spears on the rack.
5. Brush all over pastries with beaten egg and air fry for 12-17 minutes or until the pastry is golden.
6. Serve.

Variations & Ingredients Tips:

- Use puff pastry sheets instead of sheets for easier wrapping.
- Brush with an egg wash before cooking for a shiny finish.
- Sprinkle with parmesan cheese before baking.

Per Serving: Calories: 148; Total Fat: 9g; Saturated Fat: 3g; Cholesterol: 77mg; Sodium: 321mg; Total Carbs: 14g; Dietary Fiber: 1g; Total Sugars: 5g; Protein: 4g

Desserts And Sweets

Strawberry Donuts

Servings: 4 | Prep Time: 25 Minutes | Cooking Time: 55 Minutes

Ingredients:

- 3/4 cup Greek yogurt
- 2 tbsp maple syrup
- 1 tbsp vanilla extract
- 2 tsp active dry yeast
- 1 1/2 cups all-purpose flour
- 3 tbsp milk
- 1/2 cup strawberry jam

Directions:

1. Preheat air fryer to 175°C/350°F.
2. Whisk the Greek yogurt, maple syrup, vanilla extract, and yeast until well combined. Then toss in flour until you get a sticky dough.
3. Let rest covered for 10 minutes. Flour a parchment paper on a flat surface, lay the dough, sprinkle with some flour, and flatten to 1.3cm thick with a rolling pin.
4. Using a 8cm cookie cutter, cut the donuts. Repeat the process until no dough is left.
5. Place the donuts in the basket and let rise for 15-20 minutes. Spread some milk on top of each donut and Air Fry for 4 minutes. Turn the donuts, spread more milk, and Air Fry for 4 more minutes until golden brown.
6. Let cool for 15 minutes. Using a knife, cut the donuts 3/4 lengthwise, brush 1 tbsp of strawberry jam on each and close them. Serve.

Variations & Ingredients Tips:

- Use other jam flavors like blueberry or raspberry.
- Coat in cinnamon-sugar after baking.
- Fill with cream cheese frosting.

Per Serving: Calories: 320; Total Fat: 3g; Saturated Fat: 1g; Cholesterol: 5mg; Sodium: 100mg; Total Carbs: 62g; Dietary Fiber: 2g; Total Sugars: 20g; Protein: 8g

Carrot-oat Cake Muffins

Servings: 4 | Prep Time: 10 Minutes | Cooking Time: 20 Minutes

Ingredients:

- 3 tbsp butter, softened
- 1/4 cup brown sugar
- 1 tbsp maple syrup
- 1 egg white
- 1/2 tsp vanilla extract
- 1/3 cup finely grated carrots
- 1/2 cup oatmeal
- 1/3 cup flour
- 1/2 tsp baking soda
- 1/4 cup raisins

Directions:

1. Preheat air fryer to 180°C/350°F.
2. Mix the butter, brown sugar, and maple syrup until smooth, then toss in the egg white, vanilla, and carrots. Whisk well and add the oatmeal, flour, baking soda, and raisins.
3. Divide the mixture between muffin cups.
4. Bake in the air fryer for 8-10 minutes.

Variations & Ingredients Tips:

- Use grated zucchini or apple instead of carrots.
- Substitute raisins with dried cranberries, chopped dates, or chocolate chips.
- Top with cream cheese frosting or a sprinkle of powdered sugar.

Per Serving: Calories: 250; Total Fat: 11g; Saturated Fat: 6g; Sodium: 230mg; Total Carbohydrates: 36g; Dietary Fiber: 2g; Total Sugars: 20g; Protein: 4g

Almond-roasted Pears

Servings: 4 | Prep Time: 10 Minutes | Cooking Time: 15 Minutes

Ingredients:

- Yogurt Topping
- 1 container (142-170g) vanilla Greek yogurt
- 1/4 teaspoon almond flavoring
- 2 whole pears
- 1/4 cup crushed Biscoff cookies (approx. 4 cookies)
- 1 tablespoon sliced almonds
- 1 tablespoon butter

Directions:

1. Stir almond flavoring into yogurt and set aside while preparing pears.
2. Halve each pear and spoon out the core.
3. Place pear halves in air fryer basket.
4. Stir together the cookie crumbs and almonds. Place a quarter of this mixture into the hollow of each pear half.
5. Cut butter into 4 pieces and place one piece on top of crumb mixture in each pear.
6. Cook at 180°C/360°F for 15 minutes or until pears have cooked through but are still slightly firm.
7. Serve pears warm with a dollop of yogurt topping.

Variations & Ingredients Tips:

- Use honey Greek yogurt instead of vanilla.

- Substitute graham cracker crumbs for Biscoff cookies.
- Drizzle with honey or maple syrup before serving.

Per Serving: Calories: 207; Total Fat: 8g; Saturated Fat: 3g; Sodium: 52mg; Total Carbohydrates: 31g; Dietary Fiber: 4g; Total Sugars: 20g; Protein: 5g

Bananas Foster Bread Pudding

Servings: 4 | Prep Time: 15 Minutes | Cooking Time: 25 Minutes

Ingredients:

- 1/2 cup brown sugar
- 3 eggs
- 3/4 cup half and half
- 1 teaspoon pure vanilla extract
- 6 cups cubed Kings Hawaiian bread (1.3-cm cubes), 220-g
- 2 bananas, sliced
- 1 cup caramel sauce, plus more for serving

Directions:

1. Preheat the air fryer to 175°C/350°F.
2. Combine the brown sugar, eggs, half and half and vanilla in a bowl, whisk until smooth.
3. Stir in the cubed bread and toss to coat. Let sit for 10 minutes to absorb liquid.
4. Mix the sliced bananas and caramel sauce together in a separate bowl.
5. Fill 4 greased 220-g ramekins with half the bread cubes. Top with caramel-banana mixture and remaining bread.
6. Cover ramekins with tented foil.
7. Air fry two at a time for 25 minutes.
8. Let cool slightly and serve warm with extra caramel sauce and ice cream if desired.

Variations & Ingredients Tips:

- Use challah or brioche bread instead of Hawaiian.
- Add chopped pecans or walnuts to the bread pudding.
- Substitute rum for vanilla extract.

Per Serving: Calories: 543; Total Fat: 16g; Saturated Fat: 6g; Sodium: 415mg; Total Carbohydrates: 92g; Dietary Fiber: 3g; Total Sugars: 56g; Protein: 11g

Cherry Cheesecake Rolls

Servings: 6 | Prep Time: 15 Minutes | Cooking Time: 30 Minutes

Ingredients:

- 1 can crescent rolls
- 110-g cream cheese
- 1 tbsp cherry preserves
- 1/3 cup sliced fresh cherries

Directions:

1. Roll out dough into a large rectangle and cut into 12 rectangles.
2. Microwave cream cheese 15 secs to soften. Mix with cherry preserves.
3. Mound 2 tsp cherry-cheese mix on each dough piece, leaving edges clear.
4. Top each with 2 tsp fresh cherries.
5. Roll into cylinders.
6. Preheat air fryer to 175°C/350°F.
7. Place rolls in greased air fryer basket. Spray with oil.
8. Bake 8 minutes. Let cool 2-3 minutes before removing.

Variations & Ingredients Tips:

- Use other fruit preserves like strawberry or blueberry.
- Add chopped nuts or chocolate chips to the filling.
- Brush with melted butter instead of oil spray.

Per Serving: Calories: 193; Total Fat: 10g; Saturated Fat: 4g; Sodium: 245mg; Total Carbohydrates: 22g; Dietary Fiber: 1g; Total Sugars: 10g; Protein: 4g

Chocolate Rum Brownies

Servings: 6 | Prep Time: 10 Minutes | Cooking Time: 30 Minutes + Cooling Time

Ingredients:

- 1/2 cup butter, melted
- 1 cup white sugar
- 1 tsp dark rum
- 2 eggs
- 1/2 cup flour
- 1/3 cup cocoa powder
- 1/4 tsp baking powder
- Pinch of salt

Directions:

1. Preheat air fryer to 175°C/350°F.
2. Whisk melted butter, eggs and rum until fluffy.
3. In another bowl, combine flour, sugar, cocoa, salt and baking powder.
4. Gradually stir dry ingredients into wet ingredients until blended.
5. Spoon batter into a greased cake pan.
6. Bake for 20 mins until a toothpick comes out clean.
7. Let cool, then cut and serve.

Variations & Ingredients Tips:

- Omit rum for kid-friendly brownies.
- Add chocolate chips or nuts to the batter.
- Dust with powdered sugar before serving.

Per Serving: Calories: 342; Total Fat: 16g; Saturated Fat: 9g; Sodium: 109mg; Total Carbohydrates: 46g; Dietary Fiber: 2g; Total Sugars: 31g; Protein: 4g

Tortilla Fried Pies

Servings: 12 | Prep Time: 10 Minutes | Cooking

Time: 5 Minutes

Ingredients:

- 12 small flour tortillas (10cm diameter)
- ½ cup fig preserves
- ¼ cup sliced almonds
- 2 tablespoons shredded, unsweetened coconut
- Oil for misting or cooking spray

Directions:

1. Wrap refrigerated tortillas in damp paper towels and heat in microwave 30 seconds to warm.
2. Working with one tortilla at a time, place 2 teaspoons fig preserves, 1 teaspoon sliced almonds, and ½ teaspoon coconut in the center of each.
3. Moisten outer edges of tortilla all around.
4. Fold one side of tortilla over filling to make a half-moon shape and press down lightly on center. Using the tines of a fork, press down firmly on edges of tortilla to seal in filling.
5. Mist both sides with oil or cooking spray.
6. Place hand pies in air fryer basket close but not overlapping. It's fine to lean some against the sides and corners of the basket. You may need to cook in 2 batches.
7. Cook at 200°C/390°F for 5 minutes or until lightly browned. Serve hot.
8. Refrigerate any leftover pies in a closed container. To serve later, toss them back in the air fryer basket and cook for 2 or 3 minutes to reheat.

Variations & Ingredients Tips:

- Use other fruit preserves or pie fillings.
- Add a pinch of cinnamon or nutmeg to the filling.
- Brush with butter and sprinkle with cinnamon-sugar before baking.

Per Serving: Calories: 105; Total Fat: 4g; Saturated Fat: 1g; Cholesterol: 0mg; Sodium: 65mg; Total Carbs: 16g; Dietary Fiber: 1g; Total Sugars: 5g; Protein: 2g

Grilled Pineapple Dessert

Servings: 4 | Prep Time: 5 Minutes | Cooking Time: 12 Minutes

Ingredients:

- oil for misting or cooking spray
- 4 1-cm-thick slices fresh pineapple, core removed
- 1 tablespoon honey
- ¼ teaspoon brandy
- 2 tablespoons slivered almonds, toasted
- vanilla frozen yogurt or coconut sorbet

Directions:

1. Spray both sides of pineapple slices with oil or cooking spray. Place on grill plate or directly into air fryer basket.
2. Cook at 200°C/390°F for 6 minutes. Turn slices over and cook for an additional 6 minutes.
3. Mix together the honey and brandy.
4. Remove cooked pineapple slices from air fryer, sprinkle with toasted almonds, and drizzle with honey mixture.
5. Serve with a scoop of frozen yogurt or sorbet on the side.

Variations & Ingredients Tips:

- Substitute brandy with rum, bourbon, or orange liqueur.
- Add a pinch of cinnamon or cardamom to the honey mixture for extra spice.
- Serve over pound cake, angel food cake, or vanilla sponge cake.

Per Serving: Calories: 120; Total Fat: 4g; Saturated Fat: 0g; Sodium: 0mg; Total Carbohydrates: 22g; Dietary Fiber: 2g; Total Sugars: 18g; Protein: 2g

Healthy Chickpea Cookies

Servings: 6 | Prep Time: 15 Minutes | Cooking Time: 25 Minutes

Ingredients:

- 1 cup canned chickpeas
- 2 tsp vanilla extract
- 1 tsp lemon juice
- 1/3 cup date paste
- 2 tbsp butter, melted
- 1/3 cup flour
- 1/2 tsp baking powder
- 1/4 cup dark chocolate chips

Directions:

1. Preheat air fryer to 160°C/320°F. Line the basket with parchment paper.
2. In a blender, blend chickpeas, vanilla, and lemon juice until smooth. Transfer to a bowl.
3. Stir in date paste and melted butter until well combined.
4. Mix in flour, baking powder, and chocolate chips.
5. Scoop 2-tablespoon portions and shape into balls.
6. Place balls on the parchment and flatten slightly into cookie shapes.
7. Bake for 13 minutes until golden brown.
8. Let cool slightly before serving.

Variations & Ingredients Tips:

- Use mashed banana or applesauce instead of date paste.
- Substitute nut butter for the regular butter.
- Add nuts, dried fruit, or seeds to the batter.

Per Serving (2 cookies): Calories: 168; Total Fat: 6g; Saturated Fat: 3g; Sodium: 134mg; Total Carbohydrates: 25g; Dietary Fiber: 3g; Total Sugars: 9g; Protein: 4g

Spiced Fruit Skewers

Servings: 4 | Prep Time: 10 Minutes | Cooking Time: 15 Minutes

Ingredients:

- 2 peeled peaches, thickly sliced
- 3 plums, halved and pitted
- 3 peeled kiwi, quartered
- 1 tbsp honey
- 1/2 tsp ground cinnamon
- 1/4 tsp ground allspice
- 1/4 tsp cayenne pepper

Directions:

1. Preheat air fryer to 200°C/400°F.
2. Combine the honey, cinnamon, allspice, and cayenne and set aside.
3. Alternate fruits on 8 bamboo skewers, then brush the fruit with the honey mix.
4. Lay the skewers in the air fryer and Air Fry for 3-5 minutes.
5. Allow to chill for 5 minutes before serving.

Variations & Ingredients Tips:

- Use other fresh fruits like mango, pineapple or grapes.
- Drizzle with chocolate sauce or dust with powdered sugar before serving.
- Add a pinch of chili powder to the spice mix for extra heat.

Per Serving: Calories: 95; Total Fat: 0g; Saturated Fat: 0g; Cholesterol: 0mg; Sodium: 5mg; Total Carbs: 24g; Dietary Fiber: 3g; Total Sugars: 18g; Protein: 1g

Peanut Butter Cup Doughnut Holes

Servings: 24 | Prep Time: 30 Minutes (plus Rising Time) | Cooking Time: 4 Minutes

Ingredients:

- 1 1/2 cups bread flour
- 1 teaspoon active dry yeast
- 1 tablespoon sugar
- 1/4 teaspoon salt
- 1/2 cup warm milk
- 1/2 teaspoon vanilla extract
- 2 egg yolks
- 2 tablespoons melted butter
- 24 miniature peanut butter cups, plus a few more for garnish
- Vegetable oil, in a spray bottle
- Doughnut Topping:
- 1 cup chocolate chips
- 2 tablespoons milk

Directions:

1. Combine the flour, yeast, sugar and salt in a bowl. Add the milk, vanilla, egg yolks and butter. Mix well until the dough starts to come together. Transfer the dough to a floured surface and knead by hand for 2 minutes. Shape the dough into a ball and transfer it to a large oiled bowl. Cover the bowl with a towel and let the dough rise in a warm place for 1 to 1 1/2 hours, until the dough has doubled in size.
2. When the dough has risen, punch it down and roll it into a 60-cm long log. Cut the dough into 24 pieces. Push a peanut butter cup into the center of each piece of dough, pinch the dough shut and roll it into a ball. Place the dough balls on a cookie sheet and let them rise in a warm place for 30 minutes.
3. Preheat the air fryer to 200°C/400°F.
4. Spray or brush the dough balls lightly with vegetable oil. Air-fry eight at a time, at 200°C/400°F for 4 minutes, turning them over halfway through the cooking process.
5. While the doughnuts are air frying, prepare the topping. Place the chocolate chips and milk in a microwave safe bowl. Microwave on high for 1 minute. Stir and microwave for an additional 30 seconds if necessary to get all the chips to melt. Stir until the chips are melted and smooth.
6. Dip the top half of the doughnut holes into the melted chocolate. Place them on a rack to set up for just a few minutes and watch them disappear.

Variations & Ingredients Tips:

- Use different flavors of mini cups like white chocolate, dark chocolate or caramel.
- Roll doughnuts in cinnamon sugar instead of dipping in chocolate.
- Make a peanut butter glaze by mixing powdered sugar, peanut butter and a little milk.

Per Serving (1 doughnut hole): Calories: 120; Total Fat: 6g; Saturated Fat: 3g; Cholesterol: 20mg; Sodium: 60mg; Total Carbs: 14g; Dietary Fiber: 1g; Total Sugars: 6g; Protein: 3g

Boston Cream Donut Holes

Servings: 24 | Prep Time: 30 Minutes + 2 Hours Rising | Cooking Time: 12 Minutes

Ingredients:

- 1 1/2 cups bread flour
- 1 teaspoon active dry yeast
- 1 tablespoon sugar
- 1/4 teaspoon salt
- 1/2 cup warm milk
- 1/2 teaspoon pure vanilla extract
- 2 egg yolks
- 2 tablespoons butter, melted
- Vegetable oil
- Custard Filling:
- 1 (96-g) box French vanilla instant pudding mix
- 3/4 cup whole milk
- 1/4 cup heavy cream
- Chocolate Glaze:
- 1 cup chocolate chips
- 1/3 cup heavy cream

Directions:

1. Make dough: Combine dry ingredients, then add wet. Knead 2 mins. Let rise 1-5 hrs.
2. Roll into a 60-cm log. Cut into 24 pieces and form balls. Let rise 30 mins.
3. Preheat air fryer to 200°C/400°F.
4. Air fry dough balls in batches for 4 mins, flipping halfway.
5. Make filling: Beat pudding mix, milk and 1/4 cup cream

74

for 2 mins.
6. Make glaze: Heat cream and pour over chocolate chips, stir until melted.
7. Fill donut holes using a piping bag. Dip tops in chocolate glaze.

Variations & Ingredients Tips:

- Add a dash of rum or almond extract to the filling.
- Roll in cinnamon-sugar instead of glazing.
- Use different jam or curd fillings.

Per Serving (1 donut hole): Calories: 121; Total Fat: 4g; Saturated Fat: 2g; Sodium: 53mg; Total Carbohydrates: 18g; Dietary Fiber: 1g; Total Sugars: 8g; Protein: 2g

Healthy Berry Crumble

Servings: 4 | Prep Time: 10 Minutes | Cooking Time: 30 Minutes

Ingredients:

- ½ cup fresh blackberries
- ½ cup chopped strawberries
- 1/3 cup frozen raspberries
- ½ lemon, juiced and zested
- 1 tbsp honey
- 2/3 cup flour
- 3 tbsp sugar
- 2 tbsp butter, melted

Directions:

1. Add the strawberries, blackberries, and raspberries to a baking pan, then sprinkle lemon juice and honey over the berries.
2. Combine the flour, lemon zest, and sugar, then add the butter and mix; the mixture won't be smooth. Drizzle this all over the berries.
3. Preheat air fryer to 190°C/370°F.
4. Put the pan in the air fryer and Bake for 12-17 minutes. The berries should be softened and the top golden.
5. Serve hot.

Variations & Ingredients Tips:

- Use any combination of berries like blueberries, cherries, or boysenberries.
- Substitute lemon with lime or orange for a different citrus twist.
- Top with a scoop of vanilla ice cream or a dollop of whipped cream.

Per Serving: Calories: 240; Total Fat: 6g; Saturated Fat: 4g; Sodium: 5mg; Total Carbohydrates: 45g; Dietary Fiber: 4g; Total Sugars: 23g; Protein: 3g

Coconut Rice Cake

Servings: 8 | Prep Time: 10 Minutes | Cooking Time: 30 Minutes

Ingredients:

- 1 cup all-natural coconut water
- 1 cup unsweetened coconut milk
- 1 teaspoon almond extract
- ¼ teaspoon salt
- 4 tablespoons honey
- cooking spray
- ¾ cup raw jasmine rice
- 2 cups sliced or cubed fruit

Directions:

1. In a medium bowl, mix together the coconut water, coconut milk, almond extract, salt, and honey.
2. Spray air fryer baking pan with cooking spray and add the rice.
3. Pour liquid mixture over rice.
4. Cook at 180°C/360°F for 15 minutes. Stir and cook for 15 minutes longer or until rice grains are tender.
5. Allow cake to cool slightly. Run a dull knife around edge of cake, inside the pan. Turn the cake out onto a platter and garnish with fruit.

Variations & Ingredients Tips:

- Use brown rice, black rice, or wild rice for a nuttier flavor and chewier texture.
- Add shredded coconut to the batter for extra coconut goodness.
- Drizzle with coconut syrup or condensed milk before serving.

Per Serving: Calories: 200; Total Fat: 5g; Saturated Fat: 4g; Sodium: 100mg; Total Carbohydrates: 36g; Dietary Fiber: 1g; Total Sugars: 15g; Protein: 2g

Lemon Pound Cake Bites

Servings: 6 | Prep Time: 10 Minutes | Cooking Time: 20 Minutes

Ingredients:

- 450-g cake, cubed
- 1/3 cup cinnamon sugar
- 1/2 stick butter, melted
- 1 cup vanilla yogurt
- 3 tbsp brown sugar
- 1 tsp lemon zest

Directions:

1. Preheat air fryer to 175°C/350°F.
2. Drizzle cake cubes with melted butter, then toss in cinnamon sugar to coat.
3. Place cake bites in a single layer in air fryer basket.
4. Air fry for 4 minutes until golden brown.
5. Transfer to a plate.
6. In a bowl, mix yogurt, brown sugar and lemon zest.
7. Serve yogurt dip with warm cake bites.

Variations & Ingredients Tips:

- Use orange or lime zest instead of lemon.
- Add chopped nuts or chocolate chips to the cake bites.
- Substitute cream cheese for some of the yogurt in the dip.

Per Serving: Calories: 283; Total Fat: 13g; Saturated Fat: 7g; Sodium: 290mg; Total Carbohydrates: 38g; Dietary Fiber: 1g; Total Sugars: 24g; Protein: 4g

Black And Blue Clafoutis

Servings: 2 | Prep Time: 10 Minutes | Cooking Time: 15 Minutes

Ingredients:

- 15-cm pie pan
- 3 large eggs
- 1/2 cup sugar
- 1 teaspoon vanilla extract
- 2 tablespoons butter, melted
- 1 cup milk
- 1/2 cup all-purpose flour*
- 1 cup blackberries
- 1 cup blueberries
- 2 tablespoons confectioners' sugar

Directions:

1. Preheat the air fryer to 160°C/320°F.
2. Whisk eggs and sugar until smooth and lighter in color. Add vanilla, butter and milk.
3. Add flour and whisk just until no lumps remain.
4. Grease a 15-cm pie pan. Scatter half the berries in the pan.
5. Pour half the batter over berries and place in air fryer basket (use foil sling).
6. Air fry at 160°C/320°F for 15 minutes until puffed and slightly jiggly.
7. Remove, invert onto a plate and let cool while baking second batch.
8. Serve warm, dusted with confectioners' sugar.

Variations & Ingredients Tips:

- Use any combination of fresh berries.
- Drizzle with maple syrup or honey after baking.
- Serve with whipped cream or vanilla ice cream.

Per Serving: Calories: 410; Total Fat: 13g; Saturated Fat: 6g; Sodium: 168mg; Total Carbohydrates: 68g; Dietary Fiber: 5g; Total Sugars: 42g; Protein: 9g

Dark Chocolate Peanut Butter S'mores

Servings: 4 | Prep Time: 5 Minutes | Cooking Time: 6 Minutes

Ingredients:

- 4 graham cracker sheets
- 4 marshmallows
- 4 teaspoons chunky peanut butter
- 113 grams dark chocolate
- ½ teaspoon ground cinnamon

Directions:

1. Preheat the air fryer to 200°C/390°F. Break the graham crackers in half so you have 8 pieces.
2. Place 4 pieces of graham cracker on the bottom of the air fryer. Top each with one of the marshmallows and bake for 6 or 7 minutes, or until the marshmallows have a golden brown center.
3. While cooking, slather each of the remaining graham crackers with 1 teaspoon peanut butter.
4. When baking completes, carefully remove each of the graham crackers, add 28 grams of dark chocolate on top of the marshmallow, and lightly sprinkle with cinnamon. Top with the remaining peanut butter graham cracker to make the sandwich.
5. Serve immediately.

Variations & Ingredients Tips:

- Use milk chocolate or white chocolate instead of dark chocolate.
- Substitute peanut butter with Nutella, almond butter, or cookie butter.
- Add sliced bananas or strawberries for a fruity twist.

Per Serving: Calories: 320; Total Fat: 18g; Saturated Fat: 7g; Sodium: 180mg; Total Carbohydrates: 37g; Dietary Fiber: 3g; Total Sugars: 22g; Protein: 6g

Apple & Blueberry Crumble

Servings: 4 | Prep Time: 15 Minutes | Cooking Time: 20 Minutes

Ingredients:

- 5 apples, peeled and diced
- 1/2 lemon, zested and juiced
- 1/2 cup blueberries
- 1 cup brown sugar
- 1 tsp cinnamon
- 1/2 cup butter
- 1/2 cup flour

Directions:

1. Preheat air fryer to 170°C/340°F.
2. Place the apple chunks, blueberries, lemon juice and zest, half of the butter, half of the brown sugar, and cinnamon in a greased baking dish.
3. Combine thoroughly until all is well mixed.
4. Combine the flour with the remaining butter and brown sugar in a separate bowl. Stir until it forms a crumbly consistency.
5. Spread the crumb mixture over the fruit.
6. Bake in the air fryer for 10-15 minutes until golden and bubbling.
7. Serve and enjoy!

Variations & Ingredients Tips:

- Use other fruit like peaches, raspberries or rhubarb.

- Add rolled oats or nuts to the crumb topping.
- Serve with vanilla ice cream or custard.

Per Serving: Calories: 483; Total Fat: 20g; Saturated Fat: 12g; Sodium: 193mg; Total Carbohydrates: 77g; Dietary Fiber: 5g; Total Sugars: 52g; Protein: 3g

Fast Brownies

Servings: 4 | Prep Time: 10 Minutes | Cooking Time: 25 Minutes

Ingredients:

- ½ cup flour
- 2 tbsp cocoa
- 1/3 cup granulated sugar
- ¼ tsp baking soda
- 3 tbsp butter, melted
- 1 egg
- ¼ tsp salt
- ½ cup chocolate chips
- ¼ cup chopped hazelnuts
- 1 tbsp powdered sugar
- 1 tsp vanilla extract

Directions:

1. Preheat air fryer at 180°C/350°F.
2. Combine all ingredients, except chocolate chips, hazelnuts, and powdered sugar, in a bowl.
3. Fold in chocolate chips and pecans.
4. Press mixture into a greased cake pan.
5. Place cake pan in the air fryer basket and Bake for 12 minutes.
6. Let cool for 10 minutes before slicing into 9 brownies.
7. Scatter with powdered sugar and serve.

Variations & Ingredients Tips:

- Use white chocolate chips and macadamia nuts for a blondie version.
- Add a swirl of peanut butter or Nutella to the batter before baking.
- Serve with a drizzle of salted caramel sauce or a dollop of vanilla ice cream.

Per Serving: Calories: 400; Total Fat: 22g; Saturated Fat: 10g; Sodium: 280mg; Total Carbohydrates: 50g; Dietary Fiber: 3g; Total Sugars: 34g; Protein: 5g

Banana Bread Cake

Servings: 6 | Prep Time: 15 Minutes | Cooking Time: 18-22 Minutes

Ingredients:

- 3/4 cup plus 2 tablespoons All-purpose flour
- 1/2 teaspoon Baking powder
- 1/4 teaspoon Baking soda
- 1/4 teaspoon Table salt
- 4 tablespoons (1/4 cup/1/2 stick) Butter, at room temperature
- 1/2 cup Granulated white sugar
- 2 Small ripe bananas, peeled
- 5 tablespoons Pasteurized egg substitute, such as Egg Beaters
- 1/4 cup Buttermilk
- 3/4 teaspoon Vanilla extract
- Baking spray

Directions:

1. Preheat the air fryer to 165°C/325°F (or 170°C/330°F, if that's the closest setting).
2. Mix the flour, baking powder, baking soda, and salt in a small bowl until well combined.
3. Using an electric hand mixer at medium speed, beat the butter and sugar in a medium bowl until creamy and smooth, about 3 minutes.
4. Beat in the bananas until smooth. Then beat in egg substitute, buttermilk, and vanilla until uniform.
5. Add the flour mixture and beat at low speed until smooth and creamy.
6. Use baking spray to coat the inside of a 15cm, 18cm or 20cm round cake pan. Spread batter into the pan.
7. Set the pan in the basket and air-fry for 18 mins for 15cm, 20 mins for 18cm, or 22 mins for 20cm pan.
8. Check at 16 mins, cake is done when browned and set in center.
9. Let cool 10 mins before unmolding. Cool completely before slicing into wedges.

Variations & Ingredients Tips:

- Add chopped nuts or chocolate chips to the batter.
- Use mashed sweet potatoes or pumpkin instead of bananas.
- Top with cream cheese frosting.

Per Serving: Calories: 256; Total Fat: 10g; Saturated Fat: 6g; Sodium: 290mg; Total Carbohydrates: 37g; Dietary Fiber: 1g; Total Sugars: 18g; Protein: 4g

INDEX

A

Air-fried Roast Beef With Rosemary Roasted Potatoes 55
Almond Green Beans 67
Almond-roasted Pears 71
Apple & Blueberry Crumble 76
Aromatic Ahi Tuna Steaks 41
Asian Glazed Meatballs 12
Asian Meatball Tacos 26
Asparagus Wrapped In Pancetta 65
Asparagus, Mushroom And Cheese Soufflés 62

B

Baby Back Ribs 55
Bacon & Blue Cheese Tartlets 19
Bacon & Chicken Flatbread 31
Baked Eggs With Bacon-tomato Sauce 8
Balsamic Beef & Veggie Skewers 50
Banana Bread Cake 77
Bananas Foster Bread Pudding 72
Barbecue Country-style Pork Ribs 53
Basic Chicken Breasts 32
Basil Green Beans 63
Beef Brazilian Empanadas 49
Bengali Samosa With Mango Chutney 61
Best-ever Roast Beef Sandwiches 15
Black And Blue Clafoutis 76
Black Bean Veggie Burgers 16
Blistered Green Beans 68
Blueberry Muffins 5
Blueberry Pannenkoek (dutch Pancake) 2
Boston Cream Donut Holes 74
Breaded Parmesan Perch 37
Breakfast Pot Pies 7
Broccoli Cornbread 6
Buffalo Egg Rolls 28
Buttered Swordfish Steaks 36

C

Cajun Chicken Livers 35
Cajun Fried Chicken 28
Caprese-style Sandwiches 57
Caribbean Jerk Cod Fillets 39
Carrot-oat Cake Muffins 71
Cheese Straws 23
Cheesy Texas Toast 69
Cherry Cheesecake Rolls 72
Chicken & Rice Sautée 34
Chicken Apple Brie Melt 12
Chicken Breast Burgers 30
Chicken Club Sandwiches 10
Chicken Meatballs With A Surprise 27
Chicken Rochambeau 31
Chicken Schnitzel Dogs 29
Chili Black Bean Empanadas 20
Chili Cheese Dogs 9
Chocolate Rum Brownies 72
Cholula Avocado Fries 22
Chorizo & Veggie Bake 48
Classic Cinnamon Rolls 5
Cocktail Beef Bites 21
Coconut Rice Cake 75
Corn On The Cob 68
Cornish Hens With Honey-lime Glaze 34
Cowboy Rib Eye Steak 51
Crab Rangoon 18
Crab Stuffed Salmon Roast 36
Crabby Fries 18
Creamy Horseradish Roast Beef 52
Creole Chicken Drumettes 28
Creole Tilapia With Garlic Mayo 45
Crispy Chicken Cakes 8
Crispy Chicken Parmesan 30
Crispy Cordon Bleu 25
Crispy Ham And Eggs 53
Crispy Lamb Shoulder Chops 49
Crispy Pork Medallions With Radicchio And Endive Salad 54
Crispy Pork Pork Escalopes 52
Crispy Ravioli Bites 17
Crispy Sweet-and-sour Cod Fillets 45

Crispy Tofu Bites   24
Crunchy Falafel Balls   16
Curried Chicken Legs   29
Curried Potato, Cauliflower And Pea Turnovers   58

D

Dark Chocolate Peanut Butter S'mores   76
Dijon Thyme Burgers   10

E

Easy-peasy Beef Sliders   51
Effortless Beef & Rice   56
Eggplant Parmesan Subs   14

F

Family Chicken Fingers   35
Fast Brownies   77
Fiesta Chicken Plate   27
Firecracker Popcorn Shrimp   44
Fish Nuggets With Broccoli Dip   37
Fish Tortillas With Coleslaw   38
Five Spice Red Snapper With Green Onions And Orange Salsa   40
Flank Steak With Caramelized Onions   4
French Toast And Turkey Sausage Roll-ups   3
Fried Brie With Cherry Tomatoes   21
Fried Pearl Onions With Balsamic Vinegar And Basil   64

G

Garlic-lemon Steamer Clams   44
Golden Fried Tofu   61
Gorgeous Jalapeño Poppers   61
Greek-inspired Ratatouille   66
Green Bean & Baby Potato Mix   56
Grilled Pineapple Dessert   73
Gruyère Asparagus & Chicken Quiche   25

H

Halibut With Coleslaw   39
Ham & Cheese Sandwiches   7
Hawaiian Brown Rice   70
Healthy Berry Crumble   75
Healthy Chickpea Cookies   73
Herby Lamb Chops   50
Hole In One   2
Honey Mustard Pork Roast   48

Honey Pear Chips   57
Honey Pecan Shrimp   40
Honey-mustard Asparagus Puffs   70
Horseradish Crusted Salmon   42
Horseradish Tuna Croquettes   44
Hot Calamari Rings   38

I

Indian Chicken Tandoori   25
Individual Pizzas   22
Indonesian Pork Satay   53
Inside Out Cheeseburgers   16
Inside-out Cheeseburgers   13
Italian Roasted Chicken Thighs   33

J

Japanese-style Turkey Meatballs   24
Jerk Turkey Meatballs   32

K

Kale & Rice Chicken Rolls   27
Kale Chips   23
Kawaii Pork Roast   47
Kielbasa Chunks With Pineapple & Peppers   52

L

Lamb Burgers   11
Layered Mixed Vegetables   65
Lemon Pound Cake Bites   75
Lobster Tails With Lemon Garlic Butter   41
Lovely Mac'n'cheese   67

M

Maewoon Chicken Legs   32
Maple-crusted Salmon   43
Meat Loaves   49
Meatless Kimchi Bowls   58
Mediterranean Cod Croquettes   42
Mediterranean Roasted Vegetables   69
Mediterranean Salmon Cakes   37
Mexican Cheeseburgers   12
Mexican-inspired Chicken Breasts   26
Mojito Fish Tacos   43
Mozzarella Sticks   23
Mushrooms   64

N

Nicoise Deviled Eggs   20

O

Oktoberfest Bratwursts   55
Onions   66

P

Parmesan Chicken Fingers   33
Patatas Bravas   66
Peanut Butter Cup Doughnut Holes   74
Peanut-crusted Salmon   45
Pepperoni Bagel Pizzas   51
Perfect Burgers   13
Pesto Egg & Ham Sandwiches   2
Philly Cheesesteak Sandwiches   8
Pigs In A Blanket   6
Poppy Seed Mini Hot Dog Rolls   24
Pork Cutlets With Almond-lemon Crust   54
Powerful Jackfruit Fritters   63

R

Restaurant-style Breaded Shrimp   40
Reuben Sandwiches   17
Rosemary Garlic Goat Cheese   21

S

Salmon Burgers   14
Salty German-style Shrimp Pancakes   36
Sausage And Pepper Heros   9
Savory Sausage Balls   19
Scones   5
Scotch Eggs   3
Sea Bass With Fruit Salsa   38
Sea Bass With Potato Scales And Caper Aïoli   42
Seedy Rib Eye Steak Bites   47
Shrimp   35
Simple Peppared Carrot Chips   69
Sirloin Steak Bites With Gravy   48
Smooth Walnut-banana Loaf   6
Southern Okra Chips   68
Spaghetti Squash And Kale Fritters With Pomodoro Sauce   63
Spiced Fruit Skewers   73
Spicy Vegetable And Tofu Shake Fry   60
Spring Vegetable Omelet   4
Sriracha Short Ribs   47
Strawberry Donuts   71
Stuffed Portobellos   57
Stuffed Shrimp   39
Sugar-dusted Beignets   7
Sunday Chicken Skewers   34
Sushi-style Deviled Eggs   64
Sweet Nutty Chicken Breasts   31
Sweet Potato Fries   67
Sweet Potato-cinnamon Toast   3

T

T-bone Steak With Roasted Tomato, Corn And Asparagus Salsa   46
Tamari-seasoned Pork Strips   47
Tandoori Lamb Samosas   46
Tandoori Paneer Naan Pizza   59
Teriyaki Chicken Legs   29
Tex-mex Fish Tacos   43
Thai Peanut Veggie Burgers   60
Thai-style Crab Wontons   22
Thai-style Pork Sliders   15
Thanksgiving Turkey Sandwiches   11
Tomato & Basil Bruschetta   19
Tomato & Squash Stuffed Mushrooms   59
Tortilla Fried Pies   72
Turkey Spring Rolls   20
Tuscan Chimichangas   50

V

Veggie Burgers   58
Veggie Fritters   69
Vietnamese Gingered Tofu   62

W

Western Frittata   4

Z

Zucchini Boats With Ham And Cheese   65

Printed in Great Britain
by Amazon